Presented To:

From:

Date:

RECLAIMING
God's Original Purpose
for Your LIFE

God's Big Idea Expanded Edition

RECLAIMING
God's Original Purpose
for Your LIFE

MYLES MUNROE

DESTINY IMAGE® PUBLISHERS, INC.

P.O. Box 310, Shippensburg, PA 17257-0310

"Promoting Inspired Lives."

This book and all other Destiny Image, Revival Press, MercyPlace, Fresh Bread, Destiny Image Fiction, and Treasure House books are available at Christian bookstores and distributors worldwide.

For a U.S. bookstore nearest you, call **1-800-722-6774.**

For more information on foreign distributors, call **717-532-3040.**

Reach us on the Internet: **www.destinyimage.com.**

ISBN 13 TP: 978-0-7684-4136-9

ISBN 13 Ebook: 978-0-7684-8825-8

For Worldwide Distribution, Printed in the U.S.A.

7 8 / 22 21

DEDICATION

To the 7.5 billion people on Earth who stagger under the secret burden of searching for the purpose and reason for their existence.

To the family of humanity lost in the smoke of our collective confusion about why we as living creatures were placed on this planet spinning in space.

To the children and youth of our nations who are disillusioned with the trappings of religion, turned off by the disappointment of politics, and distrustful of the empty promises of science. This book is dedicated to helping you find the greatest answer for your searching heart.

To the religious and political leaders responsible for providing leadership and answers to the peoples of their nations and the world. May this book inspire you to look to the greatest alternative to national and global restoration.

ACKNOWLEDGMENTS

A book is never written by an author unless it is first written on the heart and mind of the author by thousands of contributors and influencers in his or her life and then penned through a collaborative effort of many people, who through a corporate process, deliver a product that millions can benefit from. Therefore it is impossible for any author to deserve full credit for any work accomplished.

The contributors to this work extend beyond this present generation, but include some who have gone on to the Kingdom beyond the Earth and others who still add to my growing ideas daily.

First, I wish to thank my friend, Don Milam, who continues to place demand on my untapped potential and to believe in my content to the point that he believes I am a walking library of unwritten books.

Steve, my faithful and dedicated editor, your ability to capture and convey the depth of my thoughts is nothing short of a miracle, and this book would not be released from the incubation chamber of my heart without your skill and talent.

I would like to thank Ruth, my beloved wife, and our wonderful children, Charisa and Chairo (Myles Jr.), for continuing to allow me the time to release the potential of each book and encouraging me to fulfill my purpose by sharing me with others.

ENDORSEMENT

Not only is Myles Munroe a dear friend, but someone who has greatly helped to shape our own understanding of the Kingdom of God. God is calling for us to let go of our fighting, struggling, and contending and simply embrace the truth that the Kingdom of God already reigns and rules in the earth. Pastor Myles' new book, *Reclaiming God's Original Purpose for Your Life* is like a treasure map to the promises of the Bible, teaching us what it truly means to "seek first the kingdom of God and His righteousness," so that everything else can fall perfectly into place.

Matthew Crouch
CEO, Gener8Xion Entertainment

CONTENTS

PREFACE

THE world is ruled by dead men. This statement may surprise you, but after a little thought, you would likely agree when you consider that all of the ideologies that serve as the foundations of all governments, religions, and social and civic institutions are built on dead men's ideas. Imperialism, monarchism, socialism, communism, democracy, and dictatorship are all born of ideas cultivated, incubated, and developed by men who, though long laid to rest, still live on in the practice of these ideas in our modern societies.

This book is about this unstoppable power of ideas. Our planet spins under the power of ideas, and these ideas are the source of the conditions on this Earth. Consider this: Every government in every nation is guided and regulated by ideas. All laws and legislation are products of ideas, and the social and cultural standards in all communities throughout the world are results of ideas that societies have embraced as acceptable and thus manifested in social behavior.

This book is about an idea that was introduced to the Earth by the Creator of the Earth and was lost soon after the beginning of the human journey—and has ever since been the object of the search of the human spirit. This idea originated in the mind and heart of the Creator and was the motivation and purpose for the creation of the physical universe and the human species. In this book, we refer to this idea as "The Big Idea" and attempt to prove that this idea is superior to all the collective wisdom and ideas of human intellect. It is an idea that is beyond the philosophical reserves of human history and supersedes the institutions that have governed mankind since his first human society.

The "big idea" is not a new idea. It has been imitated, disguised, misused, misinterpreted, and misunderstood by mankind throughout history and still seems to elude the wisest among us.

It is the human pursuit of this "big idea" throughout history that produced all the ideologies we have come to embrace, and this pursuit has germinated all the religions on Earth that humans adhere to. This big idea is the only answer to the deep cry in the heart of every human, and only it can satisfy the perpetual vacuum in the spirit of mankind.

What is this "big idea"? The big idea is the ideology that served as the foundation of the first and original government instituted on Earth. It is the divine aspiration, celestial vision, and eternal purpose of the Creator for His creation and humanity on planet Earth. The big idea is the concept of the ultimate governing program for mankind on Earth that provides for all the fundamental needs of humanity and produces a culture that integrates all of mankind's noble aspirations, such as equality, justice, peace, love, unity, and respect for human dignity, the value of human beings, and personal and corporate empowerment. It is an idea that is superior to and contains all the noble aspirations of democracy, socialism, communism, imperialism, dictatorships, and all religions. It is my hope that this book will unveil the beauty of this great idea that can bring the solutions to all of our earthly problems—such as war, terrorism, crime, AIDS epidemics, child abuse, environmental destruction, culture clashes, poverty, oppression, ethnic cleansing, economic crisis, family disintegration, political and religious corruption, community violence, and the culture of fear.

This book is the result of my own personal struggle for meaning, reason, hope, and understanding of life. I grappled with the inconsistencies, failures, and disappointments of man's attempts to govern himself and produce the utopia he continued to promise. I was equally distressed and disillusioned by the promises of religions, as history exposed their massive defects—revealed in their extortion of resources, trading in warfare, destructive human crusades, inquisitions, oppression, complicity in the slave trade, corruption, and more recently, serving as the motivator of terrorism and the annihilation of innocent human life. My hope in science and education was dashed as I saw the advancement of knowledge and technology become the victim of immoral application and abused by power without conscience.

Like millions, I retreated within myself, searching for answers that were not easily available within the structures and institutions that built our human society. This search led me to the most misunderstood man on planet Earth: a young Jewish philosopher who proclaimed a fresh idea that was unorthodox, unfamiliar, and untried, and challenged all of the ideas that were ever conceived by mankind. This unique idea addressed all the needs, aspirations, questions, and longings in the human experience, while exposing all of the defects, weaknesses, unreasonableness, and inferiority of our own ideas. His unique idea is so complete that it encompasses the entire spectrum of individual and national life and provides for the fulfillment of the entire human race and the planet Earth.

This idea is not some metaphysical, nebulous, impractical, cosmic philosophy that could only work in another world or that must be relegated to or preserved for some "after life" experience. Rather, it is a practical, reasonable, reachable, people-friendly ideology that is Earth-ready even though it originates in another realm. It's an idea that can work for national government, corporate business, civic life, families, and communities. It's an idea for children, adults, rich, poor, and all in-between.

I believe in this "big idea" so deeply, and testify of its evidence in my own life experience, that I have dedicated my entire life to propagating it and sharing it with every human I encounter.

This idea is not religious dogma or some narrow theological stance that isolates one from the rest of the human family. Rather, it supersedes any religious institutional position and defies the limited boundaries of all other philosophies and ideologies of mankind. This big idea is so pure that it conflicts with all of our learned theses and leads us to a frontier that appeals to the better nature of mankind.

What is this idea? It's the divine conception of the colonization of Earth by the Kingdom of Heaven—it impacts Earth's territory with the loving culture of Heaven on Earth, producing a colony of citizens who exhibit the nature, values, morals, and lifestyle of Heaven on Earth. This is not a religious idea but a global invasion of love, joy, peace, goodness, kindness, justice, patience, and righteousness under the influence of the heavenly governor: the Spirit of God.

It is the idea that humankind can be restored to the original passion, purpose, and plan of the Creator to extend His heavenly Kingdom to Earth through mankind. The celestial colony of Heaven thus fills the Earth with His divine nature, which is manifested in all human behavior. This is not religion but the manifestation of a government from another realm. What an idea! It's the Big Idea. Join me as we proceed to discover the greatest idea ever to be introduced to planet Earth. Learn why it could not come from Earth, but had to be brought here by the most benevolent King and Ruler—sovereign of a country from another world.

INTRODUCTION

DEATH can never kill an idea. Ideas are more powerful than death; they outlive men and can never be destroyed. As a matter of fact, ideas produce everything. Everything began as an idea and is the result of the conception of an idea. This book itself is the result of an idea, and the paper on which it is printed used to be an idea. The shoes on your feet, the clothes on your back, the house in which you live, the car you may drive, the cup from which you drink, and the spoon you use were all just ideas that were delivered by some human effort.

It is interesting to note, and history has proven that ideas cannot be destroyed. In fact, any attempt to destroy an idea seems to serve only to make it grow and multiply. Ideas that seem subdued or are forced to submerge in one generation will emerge in another generation and impact future ones.

The most difficult thing to fight against is an idea! Philosophically speaking, ideas can never be destroyed by physical weapons such as swords, guns, tanks, nuclear weapons, or biological/chemical weapons. Ideas may have a shelf life but can never be extinct. Why? Because they incubate in a place where no weapon can reach: the mind. If you kill a man, you do not destroy his ideas. Ideas can be transferred and live on for generations.

This is why all ideologies live on no matter what your opinion of them may be. Imperialism, communism, socialism, democracy, dictatorship, and monarchism are all ideas that cannot be destroyed, even though the men who conceived them have died. This is why even the attempts to respond to the specter of terrorism are so difficult! Terrorism is an idea peddled by extremists; this idea is sold, traded, and transferred to the minds of others and becomes the philosophical foundation of the destructive behavior that has become the greatest security challenge of the twenty-first century. How do you fight terrorism? Can a bullet kill an idea? Does terrorism die when a terrorist is killed? How do you win a war against an idea? It is my belief that the only way to defeat a bad idea is with a better idea. Ideas are destroyed by ideas.

It is my conviction that the battle for Earth is a battle of ideas. It has always been a battle of ideas. Throughout history, mankind has fought wars over ideas. The cold war was a result of a clash of ideas, as were World War II and the Korean War. Apartheid was an idea that oppressed human dignity, elevating some humans while discriminating against others; it was basically a clash of ideas about race, ethnicity, and the value of human beings. The tensions between China and the Western culture were the result of ideas. These historical issues and events were all ideological wars.

Perhaps at this point, since we have discussed so much about ideas, it would be helpful to give our attention to defining the concept of an idea. To grasp the full understanding of what an idea is, it is necessary to begin with what we call a precept. The word *precept* is a grammatical construct that incorporates the prefix *pre-*, which means "before," and the word stem, *-cept*, which means or implies "thought." Therefore, the word *precept* means "before thought" or the thought before the thought. In essence, a precept is the "original thought" that refers to the foundation thought. When a precept is conceived, it is then called "an idea." An idea is therefore "a conceived thought" that becomes the foundation of a concept, which then develops into a mental image and produces a product. Therefore, an idea can be, and usually is, the source of creation. Creation is a manifested idea.

When a thought-idea is conceived, it can be cultivated into a theory and emerge as a philosophy. It is at this stage, when an idea can become a philosophy, that it forms the foundation of a belief system. A belief system then becomes the motivator of all behavior and responses to life and environment. Belief also becomes the shade through which all of life is viewed and interpreted. In essence, ideas are the foundation of philosophy, which becomes our way of thinking, our concept of truth, and our belief system, which then produce our lifestyle and mental conditioning.

Nothing is as powerful as philosophy, and the source of philosophy is precepts, which are the ideas we come to conceive and accept. Thoughts control the world, and we become our thoughts. This is the premise on which the ancient king Solomon, over 3,000 years ago, stated: *"For as* [a man] *thinks in his heart, so is he"* (Prov. 23:7 NKJV). You cannot live beyond your philosophy and belief system. You will only change when your philosophy changes, and your philosophy will only change when your ideas change.

Part I

GOD'S BIG IDEA

Chapter One

THE GARDEN OF EDEN: GOD'S KINGDOM ON EARTH

EVERYWHERE I go, I am discovering that more and more people world-wide are tired of religion.

Not long ago I was invited to speak at an international "spiritual" conference in Mexico City. It was truly an ecumenical meeting of global proportions. Featured speakers included a leading Hindu Sikh, as well as one of the chief imams of Islam. The Dalai Lama himself was immediately ahead of me on the schedule. The Catholic Archbishop of Mexico was there, as was the Anglican Archbishop of Canterbury (from England). I was the only "Evangelical" on the list of speakers.

As my wife and I arrived in Mexico City, we were uncertain as to how we would be received. We needn't have worried. These interfaith folks greeted us enthusiastically with warm hugs and encouraging words. In fact, the woman who was in charge of coordinating everything said to me, "We know you well by reputation. Feel free to speak however you wish. Say whatever you want to say."

My allotted time slot for speaking was the last on the schedule, about three o'clock in the afternoon. All the other speakers had preceded me, and those sessions were scantily attended. I don't know what word went out about me, but when it was my turn to speak, the meeting was packed. Seated right on the front row with my wife were the Buddhist, Hindu, and Muslim leaders, all decked out in their fine robes.

As I surveyed the large crowd, I thought, *Lord, have mercy!* and then I got excited. I took off my human fear, stepped onto that stage in the power of the Holy Spirit, and said, "Stand up, everybody; we're going to pray. Let's hold hands together and agree by the power of the Holy Spirit." Everybody in that stadium did exactly what I asked. The anointing came upon me with authority, I began to pray, and something hit that arena. All of a sudden, everybody started crying. Except for the sound of soft weeping, the place was very quiet.

Finally, I said, "Be seated." By now it was so quiet you could have heard a pin drop. "Today," I said, "I want to speak to you about God's original purpose and why God made every human being." I knew I had one opportunity to speak the message they all needed to hear. When I concluded my remarks 35 minutes later, the meeting erupted in a standing ovation. Shouts of "More, more, more!" arose throughout the arena. The director came out on stage, clapping and nodding in agreement. "Give them more," she urged me, smiling.

"More?"

"Yes. They want to hear more. Please continue."

So for the next 25 minutes I told them why Jesus Christ is different from Buddha, Mohammed, Confucius, and all of the other "founders" of the world's religions. "First," I said, "let me clarify and make it perfectly clear that I am not a religious man. Second, I am convinced that the number one source of all of our problems is religion."

The place was absolutely quiet.

"Third, I am here to represent a Man who was never religious, and whose theology, psychology, and ideology are far above religion. I believe that His thesis on human manners and humanity's future is the only answer we have. After analyzing all of your other presentations, and all of the ideologies that you have presented, I proclaim that His is superior."

Although it hardly seemed possible, the room got even quieter.

"For example," I continued, "most religions say 'an eye for an eye and a tooth for a tooth,' but this great philosopher says, 'Love your enemies.'" The Muslim imam squirmed in his chair. "I came to talk about what we need the most. We don't need more religion in the world, because all of us know that we are the problem. What we need is a government in the world, and I have come to tell you about an alternative government. The only one that works is the Kingdom of God. Every single person in this room has misunderstood Jesus Christ."

I continued on in this vein for almost half an hour and concluded to another standing ovation. Why was my message so well received? Because I didn't talk about a religion. If I had preached "Christianity," it never would have worked. Instead, I talked about God, His Son, and His "big idea," and the people ate it up. Why? Because people are tired of religion. They are tired of something that does not work and cannot answer the deepest questions and longings of their soul. People all over the world are looking for something more.

Our world today is wracked by unrest and violence. War, genocide, "ethnic cleansing," and terrorism all speak to the violent clash of cultures on an unprecedented scale. At the heart of this cultural conflict lie fundamental, deeply entrenched, and thoroughly differing ideologies that are religiously based. Whenever religion becomes the foundation of a culture, then changing that culture is very difficult because it is based on a belief system. Historically, religious differences have been and continue to be responsible for most of the violent conflict throughout the world. Clearly, religion has failed humankind.

A Uniquely Beautiful Idea

Religion is man's idea, not God's.

God's original idea is much bigger and much better than anything we humans could ever dream up. And what was God's big idea? He decided to extend His heavenly Kingdom to the earthly plane, to expand His supernatural realm into the natural realm. Or to put it another way, God decided to fill the Earth with the culture of Heaven.

How did God bring His big idea into being? In this, as in almost everything else He does, God did the unexpected. Typically, human kingdoms and empires rise—and fall—through war and conquest. Not God's. Because His thoughts are not our thoughts and His ways are not our ways (see Isa. 55:8), God did something completely different. When God decided to bring the culture of Heaven to Earth, He did not use war. He did not use conquest. He did not issue a code of laws right away. No, when God set out to bring Heaven to Earth, He did something much simpler, something uniquely beautiful and wonderful.

He planted a garden.

Although invisible, Heaven is a literal place. It is a Kingdom with territory and a government—God's government. From the beginning, God had a very simple goal: to extend His invisible heavenly Kingdom to the visible Earth. This original intent lies at the heart of the Scriptures. Historically, whenever the rulers of a kingdom or empire have desired to expand its influence or territory, they have done so primarily by one of two means: outright conquest or colonization. As the sole and uncontested Creator and Ruler of all that is, God chose to expand His influence and domain from the spiritual to the natural and from the invisible to the visible by establishing on Earth a colony, or outpost, of Heaven. His plan was to populate this outpost with His own children—human beings created in His own image—who would live by and operate His heavenly Kingdom government in the earthly realm.

Unlike the pattern that would be followed by human kings and rulers throughout history, this original outpost of Heaven on Earth did not consist of an imposing fortress with thick walls, battlements, and stockades, intended to intimidate a cowed and frightened population. No, God initiated His Kingdom on Earth by planting a garden in Eden, a place specially prepared as the habitation for the first human representatives of His Kingdom government on Earth. From this hub of abundance and beauty, they would follow their government's mandate to *"Be fruitful and multiply"* (Gen. 1:28 NKJV), filling the Earth with their kind and planting Kingdom "gardens" wherever they went. In this manner, like leaven in bread, they would infuse the territory of Earth with the nation of Heaven.

UNDERSTANDING GOD'S ORIGINAL INTENT

The key to understanding humankind's presence and purpose on Earth is to understand God's original intent. If we know what God intended in the beginning, we can make better sense of where we are now and where we need to be going.

Intent can be defined as original purpose. It is more important for us to know what a person intended than to know what he or she actually said or did. If we do not properly discern intent, misunderstanding will follow. This is one reason why there are so many confused people in the world: We have misunderstood God's original intent; we have misunderstood not only ourselves, but also God's purpose for us on Earth.

Understanding intent gives us the "big picture." If we see or hear only a small part of the whole, we will misunderstand and draw an incorrect conclusion. God has a purpose for everything He does. All of us who are citizens of His Kingdom are part of His overall plan, but often all we can see is the tiny portion that involves us at any given moment. Regularly referring to the Bible, God's guidebook for life in His Kingdom, will inform us of His intent, which will, in turn, help us keep the big picture before us.

Intent is also the most critical component of motivation. It is the source of motivation and the reason why someone does something or creates something. Unless specifically stated, however, intent is usually hidden. A good example of this is a work of art by a master painter. Artists rarely state their intent plainly; they let their art speak for itself. For those who take the time and effort to search it out, the intent behind an artist's work can be discerned from the painting itself. No other explanation is necessary.

As I said before, if intent is unknown, misunderstanding is inevitable. Misunderstanding intent guarantees a waste of time, talent, energy, gifts, and resources. Unless we know what God intended, everything we do will be a waste of time. That is the problem with religion. Religion, at best, is humankind's best *guess* at God's original intent. Most religions focus on trying to get God's attention, which is the wrong approach. We already have God's attention. The key to life and purpose, however, is to get God's *intention*.

Fortunately for us, God has not hidden His intent away in some obscure manner the way an artist might in a painting. Instead, He has revealed Himself and His intent through His creation (sometimes called "general revelation") as well as through His Word (sometimes called "special revelation"). An example of the first is found in Psalm 19:1: *"The heavens declare the glory of God; the skies proclaim the work of His hands."* General revelation refers to what we can learn about God through observation of His created order. Special revelation has to do with what God reveals about Himself explicitly through either direct statement or manifestation—things about Him that we could never learn or discern on our own. The Bible is full of such statements of God's self-revelation.

In fact, God's original intention is stated explicitly in the very first chapter of the Bible:

> *Then God said, "Let Us make man in Our image, in Our likeness, and let them rule over the fish of the sea and the birds of the air, over the livestock, over all the earth, and over all the creatures that move along the ground." So God created man in His own image, in the image of God He created him; male and female He created them. God blessed them and said to them, "Be fruitful and increase in number; fill the earth and subdue it. Rule over the fish of the sea and the birds of the air and over every living creature that moves on the ground"* (Genesis 1:26-28).

The phrase "God said" indicates that what follows is the expression of the intent that God purposed beforehand in His mind. Whenever God speaks, we need to listen carefully, because we are about to receive His revealed intention.

In this case, we learn about God's intention—His purpose—in creating the universe, the planet we call Earth, along with all its creatures, and especially the human race. First, God tells us what He intended to do: create a species called "man" in His own image and likeness. Then He tells us why: so that they may exercise rulership and dominion over the Earth and all its creatures.

In order to facilitate this, God prepared a special habitat for His human representatives, a "home base" from which they would fulfill His intent and fill the Earth with the culture of Heaven:

> *Now the Lord God had planted a garden in the east, in Eden; and there He put the man He had formed. ...The Lord God took the man and put him in the Garden of Eden to work it and take care of it* (Genesis 2:8,15).

God's original intent was to populate the Earth with humankind, who then would rule and dominate the planet for Him and in His name. It's really very simple.

MADE FOR HABITATION

There are many other references throughout the Bible that also clearly express God's original intention. For example, the Hebrew prophet Isaiah states that God created the Earth specifically as a habitation for humanity:

> *For this is what the Lord says—He who created the heavens, He is God; He who fashioned and made the earth, He founded it; He did not create it to be empty, but formed it to be inhabited—He says: "I am the Lord, and there is no other"* (Isaiah 45:18).

In God's plan, the Earth has always had a purpose. God never intended to create the Earth and then leave it empty. From the very beginning, even before He formed the Earth, God envisioned it filled with plant and animal life of every variety, all of it overseen and ruled by human beings created in His image and exercising His delegated authority.

One of the ancient Hebrew psalms says, *"The highest heavens belong to the Lord, but the earth He has given to mankind"* (Ps. 115:16). God's desire was to extend His kingly rule from Heaven to Earth, but He did not want to do it personally. Instead, He chose to create humankind in His own image—spiritual beings inhabiting physical bodies perfectly adapted to inhabit the natural realm. The Earth has been given to mankind. Any religion, therefore, that teaches or emphasizes leaving the Earth to live forever in some other place in the "life to come" misses the point. If we are eager to leave Earth forever to live somewhere else, we misunderstand God's intent. Although the Bible plainly states that this present world will pass away (see 1 Cor. 7:31; 1 John 2:17), it also promises that a new Earth will take its place:

> *Behold, I will create new heavens and a new earth. The former things will not be remembered, nor will they come to mind* (Isaiah 65:17).

> *"As the new heavens and the new earth that I make will endure before Me,"* declares the Lord, *"so will your name and descendants endure"* (Isaiah 66:22).

> *But in keeping with His promise we are looking forward to a new heaven and a new earth, the home of righteousness* (2 Peter 3:13).

> *Then I saw a new heaven and a new earth, for the first heaven and the first earth had passed away, and there was no longer any sea* (Revelation 21:1).

If God's original intent—for the Earth to be inhabited—was going to change with the passing of this present world, why would He create a new one? Humankind's future in the Kingdom of Heaven will always involve the Earth—a recreated Earth.

God's original intent—and His continuing purpose—was and is to extend His invisible heavenly Kingdom to the Earth, to influence Earth from Heaven through the rulership of His earthly children created in His image. The expansion of a kingdom government (or any government) from one place to another by planting an outpost in that new place is called colonization, and the outpost so planted is called a colony. Simply stated, God's original intent was to make Earth a colony of Heaven.

I understand that most people today think of colonization in very negative terms, particularly those who have lived under colonial rule, as I have. And with good reason: throughout history almost all human colonization has been characterized by coercion, brutality, greed, exploitation, victimization, and oppression. These traits, in fact, reflect the nature and tactics of satan, the original enemy of humanity, who illegally seized control of God's original garden "colony" and deposed its rightful rulers: Adam and Eve.

Colonization was God's original idea, but unlike the human way of colonizing, His colony on Earth took the form of a garden. As an analogy, a garden shares the same general traits as a colony, but without all the negative baggage. In sharp contrast to the violent and forceful way that human empires expand, God's way was much more subtle. Just as a garden gradually, beautifully, and completely transforms the fallow ground where it is planted, the influence of God's Kingdom on Earth grows gradually and often invisibly until eventually it will fill the Earth, infusing it with the culture of Heaven. Jesus likened the process to the way yeast leavens bread:

> *The kingdom of heaven is like yeast that a woman took and mixed into a large amount of flour until it worked all through the dough* (Matthew 13:33).

He also compared the Kingdom to a mustard seed:

> *What is the kingdom of God like? What shall I compare it to? It is like a mustard seed, which a man took and planted in his garden. It grew, became a tree, and the birds of the air perched in its branches* (Luke 13:18-19).

God's ultimate goal in planting His garden "colony" was to fill the Earth with His glory. The glory of God is one of the significant themes of the Bible. For example, God told Moses, *"Truly, as I live, all the earth shall be filled with the glory of the Lord"* (Num. 14:21 NKJV). King Solomon, son of David, prayed, *"Praise be to His glorious name forever; may the whole earth be filled with His glory"* (Ps. 72:19). God reiterated this theme to the ancient Hebrew prophet Habakkuk when He said, *"For the earth will be filled with the knowledge of the glory of the Lord, as the waters cover the sea"* (Hab. 2:14).

In Hebrew, the word for "glory" is *kabod*, and the equivalent Greek word is *doxa*. Both words mean "weighty," or a "heavy weight." More specifically, "glory" refers to the full nature of a thing. God wants to fill the Earth with His full weight, His full and true nature, the fullness of who He is and what He is like. He wants to be on Earth just as He is in Heaven. Psalm 19:1 says that the heavens are filled with the glory of God. He wants the Earth to be filled the same way, by filling it with people who are filled with His nature and His Spirit.

THE RISE...FALL...AND RISE...OF A KINGDOM

Understanding God's original intent helps us understand the Bible, His written Word. Many people misunderstand the Bible and its message because they misunderstand God's original intent.

Simply stated, the Bible is about the rise, fall, and rise of God's Kingdom on Earth. It tells the story of a kingdom established, a kingdom lost, and a kingdom regained. The first two chapters of the Book of Genesis describe the establishment of God's earthly kingdom under the rulership of Adam and Eve, who God created in His own image and to whom He then gave dominion. Genesis chapter 3 tells how Adam and Eve lost their earthly kingdom, while the rest of the Bible records the working of God's plan to regain that kingdom and restore it to its former place.

The Bible begins with the Creation of the natural realm—the heavens and the Earth—but even earlier than that, He created and established the supernatural realm, which we know as Heaven, as the invisible center of His power. Heaven is God's first and original Kingdom. As a Kingdom, with God as its King, Heaven is a country just as real as any nation on Earth, even though invisible. The New Testament Book of Hebrews describes Abraham and other ancient people of faith as *"aliens and strangers on earth"* who were *"looking for a country of their own"* (Heb. 11:13-14). This does not refer to their earthly countries of origin, to which they could have returned had they so desired, but to another country in another place:

> *Instead, they were longing for a better country—a heavenly one. Therefore God is not ashamed to be called their God, for He has prepared a city for them* (Hebrews 11:16).

Heaven, therefore, is a country, a Kingdom ruled by a King: God. "King" is the only appropriate title to describe God's place in Heaven, because no one voted Him into power. God rules His Kingdom by divine right, by right of creation. Because God created all things, all things belong to Him. He alone is the rightful ruler of the universe. Psalm 103:19 says, *"The Lord has established His throne in heaven, and His kingdom rules over all."* There will never be another ruler, because God's Kingdom is eternal: *"Your throne, O God, will last forever and ever"* (Ps. 45:6a).

Since it is the nature of kingdoms to expand their territory, God decided to expand His invisible, supernatural Kingdom into the visible, natural realm. He created the heavens and the Earth and then planted a beautiful Garden in Eden as the focal point and starting place for His Kingdom expansion on Earth. He filled the Earth with plants and animals of all varieties. Finally, He created a man and a woman—human beings fashioned in His image and likeness—and placed them in the Garden as His Kingdom citizen-representatives to rule on Earth under His overall authority.

Human beings were given dominion over the earthly realm, but God is still King because everything belongs to Him. The psalmist said:

> *The earth is the Lord's, and everything in it, the world and all who live in it; for He founded it upon the seas and established it upon the waters* (Psalm 24:1-2).

> *How awesome is the Lord Most High, the great King over all the earth!* (Psalm 47:2)

When God created humankind, He gave us rulership over the Earth, but He never gave us ownership. God is King of the Earth, and Adam and Eve were its stewards, imbued with almost unlimited authority to rule in His name.

As the initial outpost of God's invisible Kingdom in the visible realm, Eden was a touch of Heaven on Earth. Everything about it reflected Heaven's culture, government, and ways. Truly, it was paradise. Unfortunately, this idyllic state of affairs did not last long. Genesis chapter 3 tells the tragic story of how a demonic usurper and pretender to the throne, through a combination of subtlety and deceit, gained control of Heaven's earthly outpost. Eden's human stewards, Adam and Eve, were tricked into disobeying their King's command, thus surrendering their earthly dominion and authority. Satan, an unemployed cherub with delusions of grandeur—and God's archenemy—seized control of a domain that was not rightfully his and quickly contaminated it with the poison of his own evil nature. Paradise was lost, and ever since, we humans have longed for the restoration of our lost kingdom.

The next eight chapters of Genesis describe the deepening corruption of human culture, morals, thoughts, imaginations, and behavior due to the sin nature inherited from Adam and Eve, as well as the continuing deadly influence of satan's evil and illegal rule.

Genesis chapter 12 begins the story of God's plan to regain and restore the earthly kingdom that humanity lost. He calls Abraham, through whose descendants He builds a nation of people He calls His own, and through whom He later sends His own Son to the Earth to reestablish His Kingdom on Earth and take it away from the great pretender.

After centuries of preparation, and when the time was just right in God's plans, Jesus Christ, the Son of God, was born to a virgin and grew up in a low-class family. Because His mission was to reestablish the Kingdom of Heaven on Earth, it is no surprise that His message was a Kingdom message, a message of colonization, as it were. Jesus' first recorded public words were, *"Repent, for the kingdom of heaven is near"* (Matt. 4:17b). His life, ministry, death, and resurrection broke the power of the pretender, restored the earthly kingdom to His

Father, and opened the door for humankind to regain our rightful place in that kingdom.

On Earth as It Is in Heaven

Jesus taught His followers to pray, *"Our Father in heaven, hallowed be Your name, Your kingdom come, Your will be done on earth as it is in heaven"* (Matt. 6:9-10). With these words, He was calling on His Father to once again restore His Kingdom rule and culture on Earth as it had always been in Heaven—and as it had been in Eden at the beginning. What was God's Kingdom on Earth like? What was life like in Heaven's earthly outpost, God's "Garden colony" on Earth?

Essentially, Eden was a direct reflection in the natural realm of Heaven in the supernatural realm. For one thing, *it had land—territory.* Every kingdom must have territory, for without territory there is nothing for a king to rule over. Although invisible, the supernatural realm of Heaven is vast and infinite— much larger than the natural realm visible to human eyes. Eden was a physical realm with physical territory. That is why God did not create man first. He created the Earth first so that man would have territory to rule. Adam and Eve ruled Eden and the entire created order, just as God ruled in Heaven.

Second, *Eden shared a common language with Heaven.* Any nation or kingdom needs a common language or else it will begin to lose national and social cohesion. Adam and Eve shared a common language with their Creator. They conversed openly and easily with Him in a completely transparent relationship and always knew exactly what He expected. All that changed when the pretender took over. Even though all humans spoke a common language with one another for many centuries—until God confused their speech at the Tower of Babel (see Gen. 11:1-9)—they lost their ability to understand and speak God's language, the language of Heaven. That is why, when we are outside the Kingdom, we do not understand what God says and no longer know what He expects. One characteristic of Kingdom life is that we can speak and understand the language of the Kingdom in a way that those outside the Kingdom cannot.

Eden also shared the laws and constitution of Heaven. These were not written down anywhere, because God had inscribed them on the hearts and minds of the human couple He had created. They knew what He expected and demanded. They understood how He wanted them to live and what He wanted them to do. God's instructions were simple: Be fruitful, multiply, fill the Earth, and subdue it. He placed only one restriction on their activities, and it was for their protection: *"You are free to eat from any tree in the garden; but you must not eat from the tree of the knowledge of good and evil, for when you eat of it you will surely die"* (Gen. 2:16-17). Aside from this one prohibition, they were completely free.

In the beginning, *Eden operated under Heaven's moral code.* Every nation must have a moral code, or else the people will become a law unto themselves and do whatever they want, resulting in chaos, disorder, and anarchy. At first, Adam and Eve had no consciousness of a moral code; they lived in perfect harmony with God. There was no lying, or stealing, or murder, or sexual immorality, or any other corrupt behavior that characterizes life in a fallen world. However, when the pretender's trickery and deceit led them to disobey God's one restriction, they discovered immediately the full weight of the Kingdom's moral code as it pressed down on them, producing a deep sense of guilt and shame.

Eden and Heaven also shared common values. Part of being a citizen of any nation is agreeing with the expressed values of that nation. In the Kingdom of Heaven, the most important value is obedience to the will of the King. Through their disobedience, Adam and Eve revealed that they no longer shared the King's values, which is why they had to leave the Garden.

The disobedience of Adam and Eve violated not only the Kingdom's moral code, but also its customs and social norms. All nations and kingdoms have *customs* (unwritten codes of conduct and expectations that have become so ingrained in a people's consciousness that they take on the force of law). They also have social norms (the manners, etiquette, graces, and standards of behavior that are regarded as normative for that society). Violation of those norms causes one to be labeled as "anti-social," and sometimes even as "criminal."

In the Kingdom of Heaven, the King's word is law, and it encompasses both customs and social norms. It is absolute and inviolable. Defiance of the King is not tolerated. Lucifer (satan) and one-third of the angels in Heaven discovered this the hard way when they mounted a coup against the King and were cast out of Heaven for their trouble. Adam and Eve made the same discovery when they found themselves banished from paradise.

In short, as an outpost of Heaven on Earth, the Garden-colony of Eden *displayed the culture of Heaven*. Culture is the culmination of all these elements: land, language, laws, constitution, moral codes, shared values, customs, and social norms. Culture defines a people. It is inherent; it comes naturally, which is exactly what God wants for His Kingdom citizens. He doesn't want us to strive to obey laws written on stone tablets or laid down in books. He wants to write them in our minds and in our hearts so that they will become second nature to us. That way, we won't have to think about living the Kingdom culture; we will simply do it.

By creating an outpost of Heaven on Earth, God wanted to establish a prototype of the original country of Heaven in another territory. Planting the Garden was a particularly apt way for God to accomplish His desire. First, the natural beauty, vibrant life, and abundant fruitfulness of the Garden are visible reflections of equivalent characteristics of God's invisible Kingdom. Heaven is a spiritual country of indescribable beauty, vibrancy, and abundance because it is the center of power for the King of the universe, who is all of those things and more—infinitely more.

Second, a garden transforms the land it occupies, turning it from barren soil into a place of beauty, provision, and purpose. In the same way, the Kingdom of Heaven transforms the natural realm, wherever the two intersect, so that the natural realm becomes a true reflection of Heaven.

God's big idea was to reproduce the Kingdom of Heaven in the visible realm by planting a Kingdom outpost on the Earth and populating it with Kingdom citizens who would govern according to Kingdom government, live according to Kingdom culture, and expand Kingdom influence until it filled and transformed the Earth. Politically speaking, the term for this kind of governmental expansion is *colonization*. As a Kingdom outpost on Earth, Eden was a *colony* of Heaven established by a righteous, just, and benevolent King who is compassionate, gracious, slow to anger, and abounding in love (see Ps. 103:8).

But Eden was also a garden. And just as kingdoms expand by transplanting their governments and cultures in another place through colonization, gardens expand through the transplantation of seedlings and cuttings onto new soil and graftings into new plant life. God's purpose was that His Kingdom citizens in Eden—His steward-gardeners—would expand the Garden and the government and culture of His Kingdom by transplanting them wherever they went.

That is still God's big idea—and His purpose for today. God is still in the horticultural business. All Kingdom citizens share a common call and commission from their King to be royal gardeners, sowing seeds and planting "gardens" of Kingdom culture and government throughout the world until *"the earth shall be filled with the knowledge of the glory of the Lord, as the waters cover the sea"* (Hab. 2:14 KJV).

Chapter Two

THE POWER OF
THE GARDEN PRINCIPLE

BETWEEN the time when Adam and Eve lost the earthly outpost of the Kingdom of Heaven to satan the pretender and the time when Jesus Christ appeared announcing its restoration, thousands of years passed. Why did God wait so long before reestablishing His Kingdom on Earth? Why did He allow so much time to pass? Why was Christ born in the particular time in history in which He appeared? Why not earlier—or later?

In answering these questions, we must understand first of all that God views time and history differently than we humans do because He is bound by neither. From the perspective of eternity, God can take all the "time" He needs to accomplish His purposes. Simon Peter, one of Christ's apostles, put it this way:

> But do not forget this one thing, dear friends: With the Lord a day is like a
> thousand years, and a thousand years are like a day. The Lord is not slow in
> keeping His promise, as some understand slowness (2 Peter 3:8-9a).

Second of all, God waited until He had guided human history to the place where optimal conditions existed for the earthly arrival of His Son and the announcement of the return of His Kingdom on Earth—what the Bible calls the "fullness" of time:

But when the fullness of the time had come, God sent forth His Son, born of a woman, born under the law, to redeem those who were under the law, that we might receive the adoption as sons (Galatians 4:4-5 NKJV).

In other words, Jesus Christ came at exactly the right time. Why was the time right? Because when Jesus appeared announcing that the Kingdom of Heaven was near—that God was once again expanding His heavenly government into the earthly sphere—those who heard His words had only to look around them to see a tangible example of the kind of kingdom and the kind of expansion God had in mind.

WHEN IN ROME...

Everywhere they turned, the people of Palestine in Jesus' day saw the pervasive, mighty hand of Rome directing their everyday lives. The Roman Empire was the most powerful kingdom in history, far outstripping in extent, strength, and splendor all other kingdoms that had preceded it. Furthermore, the kingdom of Rome was the first human kingdom to qualify as an adequate illustration and model, however imperfect, of God's plan for Kingdom expansion.

Earlier empires, such as the Assyrian, Babylonian, and Medo-Persian empires, expanded through the process of invasion, conquest, destruction, and enslavement. Their invading armies would sweep into a region, destroy its army, lay waste to its cities, tear down its infrastructure, and slaughter its people. Most of those who were not killed outright were enslaved and taken away from their own country to the home territory of the conquering power. This is exactly what happened to the Northern Kingdom of Israel when it fell to the Assyrians in 722 B.C. and to the Southern Kingdom of Judah in 587 B.C. when the Babylonians invaded.

Rome, however, followed a different kingdom-expansion strategy. Instead of wreaking widespread destruction and slaughter in a newly conquered territory, the Romans recognized the wisdom and value of preserving the people and leaving their infrastructure intact. While a Roman occupation army maintained order, Roman citizens and government officials were sent in to establish Roman government in the new territory. Their job was to reproduce the culture and society of Rome, to teach the conquered people to think, act, and live like Romans. Thus, the Roman Empire was the first human kingdom to practice colonization to any significant degree. In so doing, it also became the first human kingdom to illustrate by example the process by which God wanted to reproduce the Kingdom and culture of Heaven throughout the earthly realm.

Jesus Christ Himself certainly acknowledged the legitimacy of Rome's authority in human government. One day Jesus' enemies tried to trap Him with a religiously and politically motivated question, asking Him whether or not it was right to pay taxes to Caesar. His answer surprised them:

> *"Show Me the coin used for paying the tax." They brought Him a denarius, and He asked them, "Whose portrait is this? And whose inscription?"*
>
> *"Caesar's," they replied.*
>
> *Then He said to them, "Give to Caesar what is Caesar's, and to God what is God's."*
>
> *When they heard this, they were amazed. So they left Him and went away*
> (Matthew 22:19-22).

Later, after His arrest, Jesus stood before Pontius Pilate, the Roman governor of Judea, who asked Him if He was a king. Throughout His public ministry, Jesus never plainly referred to Himself as King because He knew the people as a whole would misunderstand. However, whenever directly questioned by a legitimate authority, He never denied it. When Pilate posed his question, Jesus answered because He knew He was speaking government to government:

> *Pilate then went back inside the palace, summoned Jesus and asked Him, "Are You the king of the Jews?"*
>
> *"Is that your own idea," Jesus asked, "or did others talk to you about Me?"*
>
> *"Do You think I am a Jew?" Pilate replied. "It was Your people and Your chief priests who handed You over to me. What is it You have done?"*

Jesus said, "My kingdom is not of this world. If it were, My servants would fight to prevent My arrest by the Jews. But now My kingdom is from another place."

"You are a king, then!" said Pilate.

Jesus answered, "You are right in saying I am a king. In fact, for this reason I was born, and for this I came into the world, to testify to the truth. Everyone on the side of truth listens to Me."

"What is truth?" Pilate asked (John 18:33-38a).

God waited to send His Son to the Earth until an earthly kingdom appeared that looked, however imperfectly, like His own, so that when Jesus preached about the Kingdom, everyone would know what He was talking about. Christ came at the right time, into the right setting, into the right culture, into the right kingdom, and into the right environment because He was preaching exactly what was happening in the world under the Roman Empire.

...Do as the Romans Do

Another way Jesus acknowledged the legitimacy of the Roman form of government was demonstrated by the fact that He used a portion of that form as a model for establishing His own government on Earth—His Church.

Whenever the Romans set up their government in a new territory, they sent a *procurator*, or governor, to rule the province in the name and authority of the emperor. At the time of Jesus' public ministry, Pontius Pilate was the procurator of Judea. In addition, the Romans borrowed many ideas of government from the Greeks, modified them, and made them their own. One of these was the idea of a "called-out" assembly of citizens who met democratically over matters of common concern. This was, essentially, the structure of the Roman Senate. The Greek word for this assembly of citizens is *ekklesia*, which literally means, "called-out ones." Both the word and the concept would have been familiar to the people of Jesus' day—the concept, because they saw it in action regularly in everyday government; and the word, because of its frequent appearance in the *Septuagint*—the Greek translation of the Old Testament that was in common use in Jesus' day— where it referred specifically to the children of God.

The *ekklesia* was an arm of government that helped the governor administer the policies of Rome. The job of these citizens was to help ensure that the policies and decrees of Rome passed down to them through the governor were enacted and enforced throughout the region of their jurisdiction.

In English, especially in English-language Bibles, *ekklesia* is translated as "church." It was this government agency (*not* a religious body!) that Jesus chose as the model for His own *ekklesia* of "called-out" followers, His government on Earth:

> When Jesus came to the region of Caesarea Philippi, He asked His disciples, "Who do people say the Son of man is?"
>
> They replied, "Some say John the Baptist; others say Elijah; and still others, Jeremiah or one of the prophets."
>
> "But what about you?" He asked. Who do you say I am?"
>
> Simon Peter answered, "You are the Christ, the Son of the living God."
>
> Jesus replied, "Blessed are you, Simon son of Jonah, for this was not revealed to you by man, but by My Father in heaven. And I tell you that you are Peter, and on this rock I will build My church [ekklesia], and the gates of Hades will not overcome it. I will give you the keys of the kingdom of heaven; whatever you bind on earth will be bound in heaven, and whatever you loose on earth will be loosed in heaven" (Matthew 16:13-19).

So Christ's Body on Earth, His Church, is not a religious body but a governmental body. Jesus' commission from His Father was to announce and reestablish the Kingdom of Heaven on Earth and to open the doorway into it through His death for the sins of humankind, and through His resurrection. Accordingly, He has commissioned His *ekklesia* to spread the Kingdom's influence, culture, and government throughout the world or, in the imagery of Chapter One, to plant Kingdom "gardens" all over the Earth to transform the world into the likeness of Heaven.

Jesus did not come to Earth to found a religion, and the *ekklesia* He established was never intended to be a religious body. Yet satan the pretender, desperate to maintain his illegal rulership over the earthly domain, has worked tirelessly over the centuries to reduce Jesus in the minds of people to a mere religious leader and His Church to a divided and largely ineffective religious institution. Both of these concepts are seriously distorted. Jesus was not a religious leader; He was a government agent on diplomatic assignment. The Church He established is not a religious institution but a governmental agency charged with publicizing and implementing Kingdom principles and policies throughout the Earth.

Jesus made this assignment very clear when He said to His followers:

> *All authority in heaven and on earth has been given to Me. Therefore go and make disciples of all nations, baptizing them in the name of the Father and of the Son and of the Holy Spirit, and teaching them to obey everything I have commanded you. And surely I will be with you always, to the very end of the age* (Matthew 28:18-20).

Contrary to popular belief, this command of Jesus, known historically as the "Great Commission," is not a religious statement. It is a declaration of government policy. And all of us who are part of His *ekklesia*, His governmental assembly on Earth, are charged with the responsibility of carrying it out. That is the purpose of the *ekklesia*. Ours is not a religious crusade. We are government appointees, ambassadors of the King on a diplomatic mission. Like master gardeners, our assignment is to replenish the Earth with Kingdom life, to reclaim, re-fertilize, and re-cultivate land that has been laid waste and made barren by the harsh, evil, and death-dealing rule of the pretender, and to fill it once again with the fresh fragrance and abundant fruitfulness of the Kingdom of Heaven.

A DISTINCTIVE PRESENCE

Wherever the Kingdom of Heaven appears it brings beauty, vitality, and abundant life and fruitfulness. This is in stark contrast to the pretender's false kingdom, which leaves nothing but death and desolation in its wake. As ambassadors of the King, we have been planted here to change the world, to make a difference by our presence. Most religions of the world, including religious Christianity, focus on getting people ready to leave this world. That is the wrong emphasis. Our mission is not to prepare for departure but to plant Kingdom gardens, to put down roots, and to plan to stick around for a while.

Why would our King place us here with an assignment to fulfill if all we were supposed to do was get ready to leave? No, His plan is to change the world through our influence, or, rather, His influence through us, and to thus transform the Earth from the waste that satan's dominion has made of it into a lush, abundant "garden" of life and beauty that fully reflects the culture and environment of Heaven. In order to bring our influence to bear, we must be present.

Many of us spend a lot of time praying for the day when we can leave, forgetting all the while that this is not how Jesus prayed. Jesus never prayed for our departure. He prayed instead for His Father to prepare us and protect us for what we have been placed on the Earth to do:

> *I have given them Your word and the world has hated them, for they are not of the world any more than I am of the world. My prayer is not that You take them out of the world but that You protect them from the evil one. They are not of the world, even as I am not of it. Sanctify them by the truth; Your word is truth. As You sent Me into the world, I have sent them into the world* (John 17:14-18).

God's plan is for the Earth to be filled with His glory. And for that to happen, it must be filled with His children, heirs, and citizens of His Kingdom who have seeded the Earth with their influence and manifested His culture. The Earth is the Lord's, and in His power, His children are going to take it back. Jesus prays not for their rescue but for their protection from the influence and attacks of the "evil one," satan the pretender, who will not yield passively to this incursion of Heaven into "his" domain.

As Kingdom citizens, we are in the world but not of it. Our homeland is in another place. We live in one culture but are identified with another culture that should make us a distinctive presence in the world. One reason that Christ's *ekklesia* has not made more of an impact in the world is because too many Kingdom citizens have accommodated and adapted to the culture of the world instead of maintaining the culture of our home government. We have neglected our "gardens" and allowed them to become overrun with weeds.

There are two kinds of people in the world: those who are children of the Kingdom of Heaven, and those who are not. Christ Himself made this distinction clear in a teaching story He told about a farmer who planted good seed in his field. At night an enemy came and planted weeds in the midst of the wheat. No one was the wiser until the wheat and the weeds sprouted up together. The farmer told his workers not to pull up the weeds for danger of uprooting the wheat as well. Instead, he allowed both to grow until harvest time, when the weeds were gathered and burned, while the wheat was stored in the granary (see Matt. 13:24-30).

When Jesus' disciples asked Him the meaning of the story, He explained it this way:

> *The one who sowed the good seed is the Son of Man. The field is the world, and the good seed stands for the sons of the kingdom. The weeds are the sons of the evil one, and the enemy who sows them is the devil. The harvest is the end of the age, and the harvesters are angels. As the weeds are pulled up and burned in the fire, so it will be at the end of the age. The Son of man will send out His angels, and they will weed out of His kingdom everything that causes sin and all who do evil. They will throw them into the fiery furnace, where there will be weeping and gnashing of teeth. Then the righteous will shine like the sun in the kingdom of their Father (Matthew 13:37-43a).*

As with many of His other stories, Jesus used here a garden-like analogy to talk about the Kingdom of Heaven. And while the overall meaning of the story relates to the end of this present age, one thing that stands out clearly is the existence in the world of two distinct cultures: Kingdom culture and the culture of the "evil one," the pretender. Just as wheat and weeds are easy to tell apart, so too is Kingdom culture distinct from worldly culture.

Our lives should leave absolutely no doubt as to which culture we live under. As Kingdom citizens, the world's culture is not our culture. If we allow the "weeds" of the world to invade our "garden," it won't be long before no one can tell the difference.

KINGDOM GARDENS BEAR LASTING FRUIT

The goal of any good gardener is to cultivate plants that produce abundant fruit. Good seed, fertile soil, proper nutrients, sufficient water, and plenty of sunshine are all necessary elements for a productive garden. Kingdom gardens, which should be showcases of Kingdom culture, are distinguished by the presence of the King Himself in the lives of His citizens. Moses, the great Hebrew leader who brought the ancient Israelites out of slavery in Egypt so they could become the chosen people of God, understood the importance of the distinctiveness of the Divine Presence. He said to God:

"Remember that this nation is Your people."

The Lord replied, "My Presence will go with you, and I will give you rest."

Then Moses said to Him, "If Your Presence does not go with us, do not send us up from here. How will anyone know that You are pleased with me and with Your people unless You go with us? What else will distinguish me and Your people from all the other people on the face of the earth (Exodus 33:13b-16).

The power of the Garden Principle derives from the presence of the Gardener. In the "garden" of His children's lives, the Gardener's presence is revealed in at least two ways: vibrant life and abundant, lasting fruit, the greatest of which is love. As Jesus explained to His disciples:

> *I am the true vine, and My Father is the gardener. He cuts off every branch in Me that bears no fruit, while every branch that does bear fruit He prunes so that it will be even more fruitful. . . . Remain in Me, and I will remain in you. No branch can bear fruit by itself; it must remain in the vine. Neither can you bear fruit unless you remain in Me. I am the vine; you are the branches. If a man remains in Me and I in him, he will bear much fruit; apart from Me you can do nothing. . . . This is to My Father's glory, that you bear much fruit, showing yourselves to be My disciples. As the Father has loved Me, so have I loved you. Now remain in My love. . . . My command is this: Love each other as I have loved you. . . . You did not choose Me, but I chose you and appointed you to go and bear fruit—fruit that will last. Then the Father will give you whatever you ask in My name. This is My command: Love each other* (John 15:1-2,4-5,8-9,12,16-17).

True Kingdom citizens are distinct from the rest of the world. This is because their lives bear the unmistakable mark of the presence of the true King, who has come to reclaim His earthly domain from the pretender, who seized control thousands of years ago. Life under the pretender's evil rule is characterized by greed, selfishness, hatred, violence, war, murder, envy, strife, lust, immorality, cruelty, brutality, empty religion, and oppression. The power of the Garden Principle, as exemplified in the lives of Kingdom citizens, brings into being a radically different environment. As we make our way in this world, planting "gardens" as we go, our lives will sow the Earth with seeds of righteousness and holiness. These will grow to produce lasting, life-changing, and world-changing fruit, such as *"love, joy, peace, patience, kindness, goodness, faithfulness, gentleness and self-control"* (Gal. 5:22b-23a).

Everyone in the world is looking for the Kingdom of Heaven, even though most of them don't realize it. People are not looking for religion. Buddhism does not satisfy. Hinduism does not satisfy. Islam does not satisfy. Judaism does not satisfy. "Religious" Christianity does not satisfy. Money and material riches do not satisfy. We were created to rule a garden domain, and we will never be content outside that environment. The King's Garden Expansion Program is designed to draw many people into His Kingdom from all over the world and to prepare them for Kingdom life and leadership in the *"new heaven and...new earth"* (Rev. 21:1) that He is already preparing.

IN WORD AND POWER

As I have said many times before, when Jesus Christ initiated His public ministry, He preached a very simple, straightforward message: *"Repent, for the kingdom of heaven is near"* (Matt. 4:17b). This was His mission statement and the only message He preached. In one village where the people tried to keep Him all to themselves, He said, *"I must preach the good news of the kingdom of God to the other towns also, because that is why I was sent"* (Luke 4:43).

Announcing the arrival of a kingdom is one thing; proving its legitimacy is another. Without the demonstrated power and authority to back them up, the words of even a king are meaningless. A king without power is only a man with a fancy title. The Kingdom of Heaven, however, is more than mere words; the eternal power of Almighty God gives it undeniable authority. Paul, a great first-century ambassador of the King, wrote, *"For the kingdom of God is not in word but in power"* (1 Cor. 4:20 NKJV). Consequently, Jesus came not only with the word of the Kingdom but with its power as well. He healed the sick. He raised the dead. He gave sight to the blind. He cast demons out of people—agents of the pretender's illicit rule—and sent them packing. He even said at one point, *"If I drive out demons by the Spirit of God, then the kingdom of God has come upon you"* (Matt. 12:28). Everywhere He went, in word and in power, Jesus demonstrated the authority, legitimacy, and invincibility of His Father's Kingdom.

One day Jesus climbed a mountain with Peter, James, and John, His three closest friends among His disciples. They spent the night there, and the three disciples heard the voice of God and saw Jesus revealed in the glory of His true nature as the Son of God. This set the stage for a dramatic demonstration of Kingdom power that soon followed:

> *The next day, when they came down from the mountain, a large crowd met him. A man in the crowd called out, "Teacher, I beg You to look at my son, for he is my only child. A spirit seizes him and he suddenly screams; it throws him into convulsions so that he foams at the mouth. It scarcely ever leaves him and is destroying him. I begged Your disciples to drive it out, but they could not."*
>
> *"O unbelieving and perverse generation," Jesus replied, "how long shall I stay with you and put up with you? Bring your son here."*
>
> *Even while the boy was coming, the demon threw him on the ground in a convulsion. But Jesus rebuked the evil spirit, healed the boy, and gave him back to his father. And they were all amazed at the greatness of God* (Luke 9:37-43a).

In the healing of this demon-possessed boy, Jesus demonstrated undeniable Kingdom power—power so irresistible that even the deeply entrenched agent of satan's government, who had successfully withstood the disciples' concerted efforts to expel it, had to flee. This little boy had been taken over by another kingdom, an illegal kingdom, but the rightful, legitimate Kingdom arrived and took him back. In the presence of the true King, the representatives of the false king had no choice but to step down and run away. Such is the power of the Kingdom of Heaven. Such is the power of the Garden Principle.

KINGDOM POWER FOR GARDEN EXPANSION

One significant element of this story of the demon-possessed boy is the disciples' inability to cast out the demon. Why did they fail? The disciples wanted to know this too. Mark's account of the same story includes this exchange:

> *After Jesus had gone indoors, His disciples asked Him privately, "Why couldn't we drive it out?"*
>
> *He replied, "This kind can come out only by prayer"* (Mark 9:28-29).

Matthew adds lack of faith to the reasons why the disciples failed to drive out the demon (see Matt. 17:19-20). Ultimately, Jesus' disciples failed because, although they knew the King, they lacked Kingdom power. They were unable as yet to operate with Kingdom authority the way Jesus did...and the pretender and his agents responded only to the authority of the rightful King.

In order for God's Kingdom-expansion plan through the propagation of Kingdom "gardens" to succeed, it was necessary for His citizens to possess the authority to act in His name. It was also crucial, however, that they not receive that authority before they were ready. In the case of the demon-possessed boy, it is clear that they were not ready—but that soon changed.

Not long afterward, Jesus decided to send His disciples on their first "independent" field assignments:

> After this the Lord appointed seventy-two others and sent them two by two ahead of Him to every town and place where He was about to go. He told them, "The harvest is plentiful, but the workers are few. Ask the Lord of the harvest, therefore, to send out workers into His harvest field. Go! I am sending you out like lambs among wolves. Do not take a purse or bag or sandals, and do not greet anyone on the road. . . . When you enter a town and are welcomed, eat what is set before you. Heal the sick who are there and tell them, 'The kingdom of God is near you.' But when you enter a town and are not welcomed, go into its streets and say, 'Even the dust of your town that sticks to our feet we wipe off against you. Yet be sure of this: The kingdom of God is near.'. . . He who listens to you listens to Me; he who rejects you rejects Me; but he who rejects Me rejects Him who sent Me."
>
> The seventy-two returned with joy and said, "Lord, even the demons submit to us in Your name."
>
> He replied, "I saw Satan fall like lightning from heaven. I have given you authority to trample on snakes and scorpions and to overcome all the power of the enemy; nothing will harm you. However, do not rejoice that the spirits

submit to you, but rejoice that your names are written in heaven" (Luke 10:1-4, 8-11, 16-20).

When the time was right, Jesus imparted to His disciples His power and authority and then sent them out to do the same things He was doing. He preached that the Kingdom of God was near; they preached that the Kingdom of God was near. He healed the sick; they healed the sick. He cast out demons; they cast out demons. Only a short time before, the disciples had experienced an embarrassing public failure in trying to evict a demon; but now they discovered that evil spirits submitted to them just as they did to Jesus. Truly, Christ had given them authority—His authority—in order *"to overcome all the power of the enemy."*

Operation of the Garden Principle requires the presence of the Gardener, but it also requires the power of the Gardener. The two go together; they are inseparable. Wherever the Gardener is present, His power is present also, which means that His influence is felt in that place. Apart from the presence and power of Christ, His disciples could do nothing. Accompanied by His presence and power, however, they could do anything He did.

That is how the Garden Principle works. God wants to multiply His Garden outposts throughout the world by multiplying His power and presence in the lives of His garden-planters, the Kingdom citizens He has appointed to spread His influence and culture wherever they go. Through delegated authority, the *ekklesia* is empowered to do the work of the King.

GARDEN IN THE DESERT

The lives and culture of Kingdom citizens should stand out from those of the rest of the world as distinctly as a garden in the middle of a desert. For centuries of desert travelers, nothing has seemed more out of place—or more welcome—than an oasis. Despite outward appearances, life hangs on in the desert, occasionally revealing itself in a flourish of vegetation and vitality, especially where an underground spring bubbles to the surface.

In contrast to the lush beauty, richness, and abundance of the Kingdom of Heaven, the kingdom of this world, under the rule of satan the great pretender, is a vast, arid desert, barren, austere, and harsh. The religions and cultures of humankind offer little to nourish the human spirit. Satan, ever the sly deceiver and trickster, lures the people of the world with false promises of hope and happiness that he never delivers. Looking for clarity, prosperity, and freedom, people find only confusion, poverty, and slavery. The things they seek cannot be found in the kingdom of this world, but only in the legitimate Kingdom, God's original "Garden" Kingdom on Earth as it is in Heaven.

Jesus Christ came to Earth to reclaim the desert and transform it once more into a great garden, the vibrant life and abundance of which reflect the character, nature, and environment of His Father's heavenly Kingdom. He was an oasis—a garden in the desert—and He planted seeds of life, righteousness, and holiness that sprouted into other oases. These were His *ekklesia*, His Church, called to plant other gardens in other places just as He had planted them. Those in turn would plant others, and the process would continue until the desert would be supplanted and transformed and only the gardens would remain.

This is the plan of God and is as sure and certain as if it has already happened. The Kingdom of Heaven has returned to Earth. The King's Garden Expansion Program is well underway, moving toward the fulfillment of the words recorded by the ancient Hebrew prophet Isaiah:

> *The desert and the parched land will be glad; the wilderness will rejoice and blossom like the crocus, it will burst into bloom; it will rejoice greatly and shout for joy. The glory of Lebanon will be given to it, the splendor of Carmel and Sharon; they will see the glory of the Lord, and the splendor of our God. Strengthen the feeble hands, steady the knees that give way; say to those with fearful hearts, "Be strong, do not fear; your God will come, He will come with vengeance; with divine retribution He will come to save you." Then will the eyes of the blind be opened and the ears of the deaf unstopped. Then will the lame leap like a deer, and the mute tongue shout for joy. Water will gush forth in the wilderness and streams in the desert. The burning sand will become a*

pool, the thirsty ground bubbling springs. In the haunts where jackals once lay, grass and reeds and papyrus will grow. And a highway will be there; it will be called the Way of Holiness. The unclean will not journey on it; it will be for those who walk in that Way; wicked fools will not go about on it. No lion will be there, nor will any ferocious beast get up on it; they will not be found there. But only the redeemed will walk there, and the ransomed of the Lord will return. They will enter Zion with singing; everlasting joy will crown their heads. Gladness and joy will overtake them, and sorrow and sighing will flee away (Isaiah 35:1-10).

The power of the Garden Principle is an irresistible power because it is the power of the King, the Master Gardener. That same power lies within the hearts and lives of every Kingdom citizen—the power to plant Kingdom gardens and spread the culture of our King and the influence of His government wherever we go. Like Jesus' story of the wheat and the weeds, we live in a world split by two competing and incompatible cultures. One is the evil, corrupting culture of a sly but arrogant usurper squatting illegally on the throne of the earthly domain. The other is the righteous, dynamic, and rich culture of the Owner, the King of the universe, who has invaded enemy territory to reclaim His own.

Many Kingdom citizens are in danger of allowing the "wheat" of their heavenly culture to be choked out and consumed by the "weeds" of the world. As we seek to carry out our King's Garden Principle, we must understand that we face an opposing culture—and we must be prepared to confront it.

Chapter Three

HEAVEN AND EARTH: A CLASH OF CULTURES

NOT long after national elections in the Bahamas, someone asked me in an airport, "What do you think about your new government?"

I replied, "I only have one government."

It doesn't matter who occupies the prime minister's chair or the Speaker of Parliament's chair or the governor's mansion; it doesn't matter who sits on the throne and is called king or queen. There is only one government, and it belongs to Him whose throne will never be moved or toppled: Almighty God, the King of kings and Lord of lords. His rule in Heaven is eternal, without beginning or end. But He also created the Earth and established His Kingdom there as well.

The Bible says, "*For the foundations of the **earth** are the Lord's; upon them He has set the world*" (I Sam. 2:8b). The words *earth* and *world* often are used interchangeably, but here they refer to two different things. *Earth* refers to the place, the physical planet on which we reside, while *world* refers to order or governing affairs. God created the physical Earth and then set on it the "world" of His government and divine order. *Earth*, then, has to do with location, while *world* deals with who is running things.

God rules directly in Heaven, but His plan for the Earth was to rule it indirectly through human representatives that He created in His own image. Adam and Eve were to rule under God's appointment and reproduce and maintain the order and government of the Kingdom of Heaven on Earth. From the beginning, the Earth was designed to be ruled by one government: the Kingdom of Heaven. Any other government is illegal on this planet. This is why the Bible makes it clear that human governments exist only by God's permission and that He ordained them for the protection of society and the common human welfare until the day His Kingdom government on Earth is fully restored. In his letter to the believers in Rome, Paul leaves no doubt as to the true authority behind human affairs:

> *Everyone must submit himself to the governing authorities, for there is no authority except that which God has established. The authorities that exist have been established by God. Consequently, he who rebels against the authority is rebelling against what God has instituted, and those who do so will bring judgment on themselves. For rulers hold no terror for those who do right, but for those who do wrong. Do you want to be free of fear for the one in authority? Then do what is right and he will commend you. For he is God's servant to do you good. But if you do wrong, be afraid, for he does not bear the sword for nothing. He is God's servant, an agent of wrath to bring punishment on the wrongdoer. Therefore, it is necessary to submit to the authorities, not only because of possible punishment but also because of conscience* (Romans 13:1-5).

Satan the pretender may believe that he runs the show and controls the governments of the Earth, but it is the King of Heaven who guides human history and destiny toward His desired ends. He raises up one power and brings down another, all in accordance with His sovereign will and purpose. Psalm 75:7 says, "*It is God who judges: He brings one down, He exalts another.*" In the Book of Isaiah, the Lord Himself declares:

> *Turn to Me and be saved, all you ends of the earth; for I am God, and there is no other. By Myself I have sworn, My mouth has uttered in all integrity*

a word that will not be revoked: Before Me every knee will bow; by Me every tongue will swear (Isaiah 45:22-23).

HEAVEN: EARTH'S ONLY LEGITIMATE CULTURE

Human empires rise and fall, but the Kingdom of God stands forever. Earthly rulers who forget or who refuse to acknowledge the One to whom they are accountable set themselves up for judgment, and even destruction. Nebuchadnezzar, king of Babylon, ruled the mightiest empire the world had ever known up to that time, but even he had to learn to humble himself before the God of Heaven:

> *As the king was walking on the roof of the royal palace of Babylon, he said, "Is not this the great Babylon I have built as the royal residence, by my mighty power and for the glory of my majesty?"*
>
> *The words were still on his lips when a voice came from heaven, "This is what is decreed for you, King Nebuchadnezzar: Your royal authority has been taken from you. You will be driven away from people and will live with the wild animals; you will eat grass like cattle. Seven times will pass by for you until you acknowledge that the Most High is sovereign over the kingdoms of men and gives them to anyone He wishes."*
>
> *Immediately what had been said about Nebuchadnezzar was fulfilled. He was driven away from people and ate grass like cattle. His body was drenched with the dew of heaven until his hair grew like the feathers of an eagle and his nails like the claws of a bird.*
>
> *At the end of that time, I, Nebuchadnezzar, raised my eyes toward heaven, and my sanity was restored. Then I praised the Most High; I honored and glorified Him who lives forever.*
>
> *His dominion is an eternal dominion; His kingdom endures from generation to generation. All the peoples of the earth are regarded as nothing. He does as*

He pleases with the powers of heaven and the peoples of the earth. No one can hold back His hand or say to Him: "What have You done?"

At the same time that my sanity was restored, my honor and splendor were returned to me for the glory of my kingdom. My advisors and nobles sought me out, and I was restored to my throne and became even greater than before. Now I, Nebuchadnezzar, praise and exalt and glorify the King of heaven, because everything He does is right and all His ways are just. And those who walk in pride He is able to humble (Daniel 4:29b-37).

To say that God is Lord of lords means that He owns everything there is by right of creation; to call Him King of kings is to acknowledge that His government and authority are above all others. All earthly rulers, willingly or not, and consciously or not, are subject ultimately to God's sovereign authority. In the end, His will shall prevail, His purpose shall be accomplished, and His Kingdom will come on Earth as it is in Heaven. The Kingdom of Heaven is the only order that God placed on the Earth. Anything else is disorder.

When satan seized control of the dominion that rightly belonged to man, he brought disorder onto the world scene: pride, envy, greed, selfishness, hatred… and man-centered religion, which reduces the life-giving principles of God's Kingdom to empty rites, rituals, and rules.

The point of all of this is to make it clear that the culture of Heaven is the only legitimate culture for the Earth. So-called human culture, which is influenced and controlled by satan, and therefore is in conflict with the culture of Heaven—is an illegitimate culture. So we have two cultures in conflict, a cultural clash between Heaven and Earth.

Culture Problems

Anyone who pays any attention at all to human events at home or abroad knows that global society is in upheaval of unprecedented proportions. We face many global challenges that we just can't solve. The United Nations was formed after the Second World War for the purpose of preventing war. Yet in the 60 years of its existence, there have been more wars than in all the rest of recorded human history. So even our best and most well-intentioned attempt to prevent ourselves from killing each other has failed. Even worse, corruption scandals in recent years have revealed that there are those within the UN itself who have placed their own enrichment ahead of the greater good and engaged in ongoing activities that have undermined the very goals the organization is trying to achieve.

If we judge only by what we see happening around us and around the world every day, how can we help but become frustrated, discouraged, and even fearful? Who among us does not wake up in the morning, glance at the news headlines or listen to broadcast news reports, and immediately become depressed? We are all looking and dreaming and hoping and praying for a better world, aren't we? Imagine what it would be like to get up one morning and find no news of war, or genocide, or ethnic cleansing, or terrorism, or starvation, or poverty. Unfortunately, truly good news like that is an increasingly rare commodity in our world today.

Strangely enough, the single biggest cause of our problems is the very thing that was supposed to provide a solution: religion. Historically, religion has been the primary driving force behind the vast majority of global conflict. This is especially true today. Global terrorism is fueled by extremist religious ideology. In the name of Allah, radical Muslim groups such as Hamas and al-Qaida utilize violence and terror to either convert or destroy the "infidels" (unbelievers). In Iraq, Sunni and Shiite Muslims kill each other in a bloodletting unleashed by the release of years of pent-up anger, resentment, hostility, and hatred. The burning of churches in Pakistan results in the retaliatory torching of temples and mosques in India.

Religion is *not* a peaceful prospect. And religious conflict is not restricted to Islam or Hinduism or other "non-Western" religions. Christianity carries its own heavy burden of responsibility for religiously motivated conflict. The Crusades of the Middle Ages and centuries of hostility and persecution between Catholics and Protestants are two prime examples. Think of all the years that

Belfast and Northern Ireland burned with unrest and violence because Catholics and Protestants were unable to live together in peace. Denominations within the Church are like little kingdoms of their own, jockeying for position and advantage and fighting amongst themselves over theology, doctrine, and theories of church government instead of working together for the common cause of the Gospel. This is why I make a clear and unambiguous distinction between the Kingdom of Heaven and institutional Christianity as a religious entity. They are not the same.

The shrinking of our global community through telecommunications technology and the Internet has greatly accelerated the rate and intensity of culture clash. A "take-no-prisoners" war is being waged for the soul of our culture, and it is vitally important that we identify the nature of the fight. What do we do when a major newsmagazine runs a cover story titled "Muslims in the USA" or we discover that mosques are popping up next to churches all over America? It is a clash of cultures. How should we respond to the debate in England over whether or not female religious devotees can wear veils in school or for driver's license photographs, even though the teachers and government officials need to be able to see their faces to identify them? It is a clash of cultures. The need to preserve democratic freedom and individual rights conflicts with the need for greater security.

What do we do when the counterculture of sexual perversion labors and lobbies vigorously to dignify and legitimize itself through legislation? How should we respond to the claim that two men or two women should be able to marry each other, and even to raise children in such a same-gender household? What do we do when we claim to believe in "family values" only to discover that society has redefined *family* to mean anything anybody at all wants it to mean? This is no time to play religious games; the very life of our culture is at stake.

What do we do when 70 bishops in a major American denomination vote to ordain an openly and active gay priest as archbishop of an entire diocese? What do we do? We can't afford to remain silent. One of the worst things in the world is for people who know what is right to remain silent in the face of wrong. We need help from beyond ourselves—help from the Creator of the Earth's original and only legitimate culture.

THE POWER OF CULTURE

Culture is stronger than politics. It really doesn't matter who is in power. Politicians come and go, and governments rise and fall, but culture still remains. Culture is also more powerful than religion. One of the biggest challenges that Church leaders faced during the first few centuries of the Church's existence was how to keep those who were coming into the Church out of pagan backgrounds from bringing elements of their pagan culture with them and blending these with their new faith in Christ. Even today we continue to see the enormous power of culture in the fact that many believers and Kingdom citizens display lifestyles that differ little from those of people who make no claim to be in the Kingdom.

The United States of America has a rich historical heritage of faith and even today has the highest percentage of citizens who claim to be believers (Christians) of any of the industrialized nations. Yet every year in America, 500,000 unborn babies are aborted—*legally*. The most progressive nation in the world murders half a million babies in the womb every year, and the law protects both the mothers who choose to kill their children as well as the doctors who carry out the destruction. This is insanity, yet it exemplifies the power of culture over religion in its ability to shape the thoughts, values, and beliefs of people and to influence their behavior and what they are willing to accept.

In another example, gay rights activists in America have made great strides forward in their efforts to legitimize their lifestyle through the legal process. Gay marriage is already legal in the states of Massachusetts and California, and efforts to legalize it in other states are on the rise. An increasing number of Americans—many of the same ones who claim faith in Christ—say they find nothing wrong with homosexual relationships and that gays should be afforded special "civil rights" protection under the law. Legislation has even been proposed that would make anti-gay speech or activity a hate crime.

I am not picking on America here but just illustrating the power of culture over religion—even in a nation that is still widely regarded as the most "religious" nation in the industrialized world. Similar developments are taking place in other parts of the globe. We are smarter but not wiser. We are in a pitched battle for the culture of the Earth. Most often what we assume to be issues of social, religious, or political activity are really issues of culture.

Culture is the manifestation of the collective thinking of a people. This means that whoever controls the minds of the people creates and controls the culture. Culture is also a product of law. The most effective way to change a culture is to control its laws, because whatever is instated into law eventually will become accepted as "normal" by most citizens, regardless of how they might have felt at the beginning. This is all part of the process of mind control.

Is it any surprise then that when God got ready to create a nation out of people who had been slaves for 400 years, He gave them a code of law encapsulated in the Ten Commandments? God knew that before the Israelites could become a holy nation and a people set apart for Him, He had to change their thinking. His purpose was to create a Kingdom culture on Earth by raising up a nation of Kingdom thinkers and Kingdom livers.

This is why the Bible says that the law of God is good. When we obey the law of God, we are producing the culture of Heaven. This has nothing to do with practicing a religion, but rather with instating a culture based on the law of God that will permeate and transform every part of society. Paul described what it meant to exchange the world's culture for the culture of Heaven when he wrote,

> Do not conform any longer to the pattern of this world, but be transformed by the renewing of your mind. Then you will be able to test and approve what God's will is—His good, pleasing, and perfect will (Romans 12:2).

To renew our minds means to take on the attitude of Christ (see Phil. 2:5) and to understand that as believers and Kingdom citizens we have the mind of Christ (see I Cor. 2:16). We need to know His mind and discern His thinking. Taking up the culture of Heaven means learning to think God's thoughts and living accordingly.

The Kingdom of God is a kingdom of the heart and mind that manifests itself in culture. The secret to expanding Heaven's culture on Earth is to change people's minds, to cultivate them like a garden, carefully seeding their minds with the thoughts, beliefs, ideals, values, and convictions of Heaven. The end result will be the transformation of an arid, spiritually barren mental landscape into a verdant and vibrant garden full of life, hope, and unlimited potential.

In contrast to the world's culture, which, reflecting the character and nature of the pretender, is a culture of desperation, discrimination, depravity, division, destruction, and death, Heaven's culture is a culture of power, provision, and possibility. This is the culture of the King, of whom Paul writes,

Now to Him who is able to do immeasurably more than all we ask or imagine, according to His power that is at work within us, to Him be glory in the church and in Christ Jesus throughout all generations forever and ever! Amen (Ephesians 3:20-21).

God wants us to become all that we can be, and He has the power to enable us to succeed.

DECLARATION OF INDEPENDENCE

The Kingdom of Heaven is not a religion; it is a government and a society with a culture that is just as real as any devised by man—but even more so. That is why God issued laws for us to obey in His Kingdom. Those laws produce a lifestyle, and that lifestyle manifests in a culture, in a community that creates a society that is totally unique. This is the culture that existed in the Garden of Eden, and the culture that all Kingdom citizens are to reproduce and manifest in the "gardens" of our lives as we put the Garden Principle into operation throughout the world.

Given enough time and influence, one culture can supplant another. For example, although the vast majority of Bahamian citizens are of African descent, ours is not an African culture. Visitors to our beautiful Caribbean country notice immediately that they are surrounded by the culture of Great Britain. We drive on the left side of the road, we traditionally drink tea rather than coffee, and, for many years, dressed in a "traditional" suit consisting of short pants, long socks, a long-sleeved jacket, and long necktie. For the longest time I could not understand why we wore ties in 90-degree weather, until I visited England, where it is always cold.

During the centuries when our country was a colony of Great Britain, the cultures of these islands and of our original African heritage were completely transformed by British culture. Every vestige of African or Caribbean culture was removed until today. Although we may look like Africans, we dress like the British, speak like the British, and act like the British. Even our system of government resembles that of England. One culture transformed and supplanted another.

Anyone can identify our culture by the way we look, speak, and act. Kingdom culture should be the same way. If we are Kingdom citizens, our culture should be evident to everyone we come in contact with. Worldly culture says, "Homosexual marriage is just as valid as heterosexual marriage." Kingdom culture says, "Marriage is exclusively a male-female relationship." Worldly culture says, "Have sex as often as you like with whomever you wish without guilt and without commitment." Kingdom culture says, "Reserve sex for the marriage relationship alone, and then stay married to the same spouse for life." Worldly culture says, "Live for the moment. Watch out for 'number one,' and make sure you grab your piece of the pie." Kingdom culture says, "Live with eternity in view, treat others the way you would like them to treat you, and put the interests of others ahead of your own."

It was never God's desire or intent that there be a British culture, or an American culture, or a Bahamian culture, or a Jamaican culture, or a French culture, or a Chinese culture. He wanted a Kingdom culture, one culture throughout the entire created realm. This is why Christ taught us to pray, "*Your kingdom come, your will be done on earth as it is in heaven*" (Matt. 6:10). God wants Earth to reflect Heaven.

Culture rests on the foundation of law. God's laws are not to restrict us but to protect us and to ensure that His culture fills the Earth. This is what Adam and Eve forgot when they chose to rebel against the King in Eden. When they ate of the one tree in the Garden that God had placed off-limits, they did more than commit personal sins for the sake of pleasure and enlightenment; theirs was an act of treason against the government of their Creator. Their disobedience was, in fact, a declaration of independence from God and His righteous, loving, and benevolent rule. Adam and Eve turned their backs on God's Kingdom in favor of setting up a regime of their own making. Unfortunately, satan the pretender illegally seized the throne, began pulling the strings, and imposed his own culture of hatred, murder, and deceit.

It is no accident, then, that one of the first recorded events in this new illegitimate kingdom was an act of brother-against-brother murder. When Cain killed his brother Abel (see Gen. 4:1-16), he was simply reflecting his culture. And today, thousands of years and millions of deaths later, brother still kills brother in every nation, city, and town on Earth. It is part of our culture.

In the beginning, Adam and Eve ruled the Garden realm through the presence of the Spirit of God. When they declared their independence, the Holy Spirit departed and returned to Heaven, the home country. Man was on his own and at the mercy of the pretender. But God loved man too much to leave him on his own and with his original destiny unfulfilled. He did not leave us to fend for ourselves, spinning through space, lost in our own confusion. He said, "They may have declared their independence, but they will never survive without Me. I'm going to return to My own earthly territory and reclaim it, and them, whom I love. I planted a Garden there once. Now I will replant My Garden, but this time I will plant it in the hearts of My people, from where it will spread to the ends of the Earth."

Restoring What the Pretender Stole

God's purpose in re-establishing His Kingdom on Earth through the life, death, and resurrection of His Son is to dethrone the pretender, kick him out of the territory, and restore what he stole from the people he has tyrannized through the ages. If we want to know what kind of ruler satan has been in his illegal regency of the earthly realm, all we have to do is look around us at the generally deplorable state the world is in spiritually, morally, and ethically. If we want to know what the pretender's rule is like, all we have to do is review any of the abundant examples from history of despotic dictators and self-serving tyrants who raped the land, robbed its resources, and victimized its citizens for their own enrichment. And if we want to understand what the pretender stole from us, all we have to do is examine the common results of human colonization. As a case in point, let's consider my own nation of the Bahamas.

As I said before, my country was a colony of Great Britain for over 200 years. We were British subjects, and the British government did everything it could to make us dress, speak, and act accordingly. They even sent a governor and other political officials to administer and enforce British law in the colony. I am not suggesting that all or even most of these people were evil or had evil intent, but their presence and work in the name of the British crown had a profound impact on the Bahamian people.

Over the course of more than two centuries, a succession of governors took away from us three important ingredients of our identity as a people and replaced them with those of the home government. The first thing the governor took away from us was our *language*. Even though most Bahamians are of African descent, we do not speak African languages or dialects. We speak "the King's English" (or the Queen's).

In the same way, when the pretender took over Adam and Eve's domain, he stole their language—our ability to communicate intimately and personally with our Creator. He took away our ability to talk to God, and as a race we have been trying desperately to get it back ever since. This is why, when we become Kingdom citizens through faith in Jesus Christ, one of first things He does is restore our original language, enabling us to talk intimately, personally, and directly to God once again in a way that is not possible outside the Kingdom.

The second thing the governor took from us was our *history*. It was his job to teach us the history of the ruling kingdom, so instead of learning about Shaka Zulu and other leaders and events of African history and heritage, we learned about King Henry VIII and his six wives. We learned about Sir Francis Drake, Queen Elizabeth, and "Bloody Mary" Tudor. We studied Shakespeare. We learned about Oliver Cromwell and about the English Civil War, and thus we lost the sense of our own history.

Likewise, when the pretender seized control, he stole our knowledge of our history as a race. We forgot who we are and where we came from. We lost any sense of awareness of the Kingdom from which we originated and of the King who fashioned us in His own image. This too was restored when Christ reestablished the Kingdom of Heaven on Earth. When we first enter the Kingdom, we come to Christ with a history of sin, rebellion, and estrangement from God. Christ takes that away and gives us a new "history" of salvation, forgiveness, joy, and peace. He restores us to our rightful place as sons and daughters of the King.

Finally, the third thing the colonial governor took from us was our *culture*. We started drinking tea with chocolates three times a day. And even though few of us had ever been to England, we began each school day waving little British flags and singing, "Rule Britannia." We sang to a queen and country we had never seen. In thousands of ways every day we were surrounded by, exposed to, taught, and indoctrinated in the ways and customs of British culture until virtually all traces of any indigenous African or Caribbean culture disappeared.

The same thing happened to humankind under the pretender's rule. The more his spirit of evil permeated human society, and the more our human hearts departed from God and His ways, the more we took on the traits of the pretender's depraved and decadent culture, and the less we remembered the righteousness, peace, joy, and abundance of the culture of Heaven. Christ came to restore all of that. When we become Kingdom citizens, He gives us a new nature to supplant our old, corrupt, sinful nature—a new nature that loves God and delights to do His will and that understands, desires, and has the power to live according to Kingdom culture.

Christ came to give us back what the pretender stole. We are talking about a complete change of culture. We cannot be in the Kingdom of God and continue to live the way we used to live. When His Kingdom takes over our lives, everything changes.

The colonial governor of the Bahamas lived in a large pink house built by the British, and when we declared our independence, he returned to England. The Governor of God's Kingdom on Earth, on the other hand, will never be evicted and sent home because He does not reside in a physical building. Acts 17:24 says, "*The God who made the world and everything in it is the Lord of heaven and earth and does not live in temples built by hands.*" Instead, through His Holy Spirit, He dwells in the hearts and lives of the citizens of His Kingdom.

THE RETURN OF THE KING

One of the biggest problems most of us face as believers and Kingdom citizens is that we try to reproduce the new Kingdom culture with our old, un-renewed minds. Our minds have already been tainted and corrupted by worldly culture, which makes our efforts to create good government, promote clean living, and improve society largely ineffectual at best. It is impossible to draw fresh water from a bitter source.

When Christ came to Earth to restore His Father's Kingdom, the first thing He had to do was clean house. Before He could send His Spirit to dwell in us,

He had to wash away the filth He found there: the sin, immorality, degradation, evil, bitterness, envy, jealousy, anger, deceit, gluttony, greed, sexual perversion, prejudice, hatred, and lust. His death on the cross was the cleanup program. His blood has the power to wash away all the filth and degradation of the pretender and his evil rule. Christ came to wash us free of our sins in order to prepare the "house" of our bodies for the return of the Royal Governor so that Heaven's culture—our original culture—can come back.

Jesus made it clear that restoring the Kingdom and reinstating its culture on Earth had nothing to do with buildings when He said,

> The kingdom of God does not come with your careful observation, nor will people say, 'Here it is,' or 'There it is,' because the kingdom of God is within you (Luke 17:20b-21).

But before the Kingdom can be within us, we must be thoroughly cleansed from the inside out so that the Holy Spirit can inhabit a holy temple. We are not talking about religion here but about the return of legitimate government. The Holy Spirit dwelling in us means that the entire government of Heaven is on the Earth today. This is what Jesus meant when He said that the Kingdom of God is within us.

The Kingdom of Heaven has been reinstated in the territory stolen by the pretender, and it will continue to gain ground. A royal Garden has bloomed in the desert and is spreading inexorably and irresistibility over the barren ground, preparing the way for the day when the King Himself will return visibly and powerfully to take His throne. At that time, the Earth will be filled with the knowledge of His glory, as the waters cover the sea (see Hab. 2:14).

The culture of God must come back to Earth. He has called us and commissioned us to make a difference in the world. It is time for Kingdom citizens everywhere to infuse this sick world with the curative elixir of the culture of Heaven. Our King has placed us here to seed worldly government with the government of the Kingdom. He has called us to invade the culture of worldly business with the business of Heaven. This is not about profit but about permeation. Like yeast, we are to infiltrate and permeate the world with Kingdom culture until the whole is transformed—until the barren desert is a beautiful, fertile, and fruitful garden once more.

The Kingdom of Heaven is not about escaping Earth; it is about occupying the planet. As Kingdom citizens, we are destined to change the world. In the name of Jesus the King, nations and peoples will be set free from the cruel bondage and deadly culture of satan the pretender. The time of the Kingdom of God is upon us. Let His Kingdom come. Let His will be done on Earth as it is in Heaven. Let us live according to His laws and principles. Let His culture reign supreme. Let the Earth be filled with His glory.

Chapter Four

THE MASTER GARDENER: THE KEY TO A SUCCESSFUL GARDEN

GARDENS are marvelous things. It is truly amazing how even a little plot of carefully cultivated fruit trees, vegetable plants, or brightly colored flowers can totally transform an otherwise drab and ordinary landscape. More than almost anything else on Earth, a well-cared-for garden signals the presence of life in its fullest abundance, vitality, and beauty.

The Islands of the Bahamas are the home of many beautiful gardens, both public and private. Most Bahamians take great pride in doing everything possible to make our nation a true island paradise of botanical richness and splendor. Of course, the same is true in many other parts of the world. There is something about a garden that stirs an inner chord in the spirit of most of us, a chord of peace, harmony...and *rightness*, as if to say, "This is the way nature is supposed to be." And of course, that is true.

Every garden needs a gardener, someone to till the soil, sow the seeds, nurture the young plants, and prune, shape, and groom them for maximum fruitfulness and productivity. It must be someone who truly has a heart for the garden, someone who loves it and is completely committed to its growth and success. Even the Garden of Eden, God's original Kingdom outpost on Earth, needed a gardener. God did not create the Garden and leave it to fend for itself. A gardener was necessary to tend it, nurture it, and ensure that it fulfilled all of God's will and desires for it.

God placed Adam and Eve in the Garden as its stewards and caretakers, king and queen of the earthly domain. They were gardeners, certainly, but neither of them was the Master Gardener. Until the day they disobeyed God, lost their position, and had to leave, Adam and Eve worked in close concert and harmony with the true Master Gardener of Eden—the Holy Spirit of God—who, unlike them, had been present and intimately involved in its creation. Read the opening words of the Bible, the constitution of the Kingdom of Heaven:

> *In the beginning God created the heavens and the earth. Now the earth was formless and empty, darkness was over the surface of the deep, and the Spirit of God was hovering over the waters* (Genesis 1:1-2).

The Spirit of God was present and was the primary agent in the creation of the physical realm, including the Garden of Eden. Using similar language, the apostle John reiterates this truth:

> *In the beginning was the Word, and the Word was with God, and the Word was God. He was with God in the beginning. Through Him all things were made; without Him nothing was made that has been made* (John 1:1-3).

Although John's reference to the "Word" through whom "all things were made" refers to Jesus Christ, the Son of God, the Spirit of God is also the Spirit of Christ, because they are all of one essence—one God in three Persons. By right and agency of creation, the Holy Spirit was the Master Gardener of Eden, the Governor of God's original colony on Earth. Like human colonial governors, He guides and oversees the lives and welfare of His citizens. Unlike His human counterparts, however, who live in fancy houses and mansions made with human hands, the Governor of the Kingdom lives in the hearts and lives of His citizens. As He was in Eden, He is still the Master Gardener, overseeing the planting, growth, fruitfulness, and reproduction of Kingdom "gardens" in the lives of Kingdom citizens and throughout the world.

All of us who are believers and citizens of the Kingdom of Heaven are immigrants on this planet. God placed us here to fill the Earth with His government and glory, but He did not abandon us to do so on our own. The Bible says that He is a God of order, not disorder. This means also that He is a God of government, not anarchy. As we saw in the last chapter, when God rescued the Israelites from slavery in Egypt in order to make them into a nation, the first thing He did was give them a government encoded in law: the Ten Commandments.

In the same way, He has placed the Holy Spirit as the Governor of His children and citizens, to ensure that the "gardens" of our lives grow in a cultivated, orderly, and disciplined manner for maximum fruitfulness, in accordance with Kingdom principles, rather than grow wild and reckless with no direction or control. Proverbs 29:18 says, *"Where there is no revelation, the people cast off restraint; but blessed is he who keeps the law."* The Holy Spirit, our Master Gardener, is the one who reveals to us the will and ways of our King and teaches us how to live a Kingdom lifestyle and to manifest Kingdom culture. He is essential to our assignment of building the community of Heaven on Earth. His major role is to transform the earthly realm into the heavenly realm.

THE HOLY SPIRIT ENACTS GOD'S WILL

The Bible is about a King, His Kingdom, and His royal family. It is a royal document chronicling the purposes, desires, and decrees of the King, as well as the activities, past history, and future destiny of His children and heirs. It also describes the King's expansion program, His plan to expand His heavenly realm into earthly territory. As we saw in Chapter One, He did this by establishing an outpost—a Garden—in Eden. Then He created a man and a woman and put them there as caretakers and administrators—rulers of the physical earthly realm just as He Himself ruled in Heaven. Theirs was not to be an independent rule, however, so He appointed a Governor to oversee the overall expansion program. And who better for Governor than His own Spirit, who knows His mind intimately and perfectly? In addition, this Governor could work in close harmony with the human administrators who, as spirit beings clothed in an earthen shell, could commune with Him spirit to Spirit.

As Governor and Master Gardener, the Holy Spirit's primary role is to execute and enact the will of the King who owns the Garden and everything and everyone in it. Under a democratic system of government, a governor is elected by the people, who also have the power to remove him or her from office. A kingdom is not a democratic system, however, and this is especially true of the Kingdom of God. In a kingdom, the king's word is law and his will is absolute. The king appoints governors to oversee the various territories and regions of his kingdom—and only he can remove them.

This is exactly how government administration worked in the Roman Empire, which is one reason it was such an ideal model to serve as a backdrop for Christ's message of the Kingdom of Heaven. During Christ's earthly ministry, Pontius Pilate was the Roman governor of Judea, appointed by Tiberias Caesar, the emperor. Although Pilate proved to be a very unpopular governor, the people of Judea had no power to remove him. The most they could do was petition the emperor to recall and replace him, which they did in A.D. 36.

Carrying out the will of the king is the paramount responsibility of the governor. The big difference between a king and a prime minister or a president is that the latter two cannot always have their will or way in the country. They have to negotiate with Parliament or Congress. They have to debate and discuss, and often make compromises just to get part of what they want. Even then, the final legislation is subject to judicial review and can be overturned if it is judged to violate the constitution.

In contrast, a king's word *is* the constitution. His word is law, and as such is inviolable. It is not open to debate, discussion, or reversal. In a kingdom, the king imposes his personal will on the citizens, and it becomes policy. The role of the governor is to implement that same policy in all the king's territory that is under the governor's jurisdiction. Whenever the governor speaks in his official capacity, his word carries the authority of the king because it is the word of the king, and the king's word is law. In Judea during Jesus' day, whenever Pilate issued a decree or made a proclamation, it carried the same force of law as if the Roman emperor himself had delivered it in person.

THE HOLY SPIRIT ASSERTS GOD'S AUTHORITY

Governors in a kingdom are personal appointees of the king. They may be personal friends of the king, or at least known to him by reputation or recommendation. Either way, they are chosen for their loyalty to the king and their commitment to his policies. His purpose is their purpose, and his objectives, their objectives. Quite often they come from the very center of the king's court, intimates of the king who understand his thoughts and are of one mind with him.

This certainly describes the Holy Spirit, who never speaks of His own accord, but says only that which He has received from God the Father, the King of Heaven. He is perfectly suited to be Governor of Heaven's Kingdom gardens on Earth because He knows perfectly the heart and mind of the King. This intimacy enables Him to conform the hearts and minds of Kingdom citizens to those of the King, thus shaping the "gardens" of their lives to faithfully manifest the government and culture of Heaven. In the words of Paul:

> *In the same way, the Spirit helps us in our weakness. We do not know what we ought to pray for, but the Spirit Himself intercedes for us with groans that words cannot express. And He who searches our hearts knows the mind of the Spirit, because the Spirit intercedes for the saints in accordance with God's will* (Romans 8:26-27).

Jesus Himself was even more explicit in describing the work of the Master Gardener:

And I will ask the Father, and He will give you another Counselor to be with you forever—the Spirit of truth. The world cannot accept Him, because it neither sees Him nor knows Him. But you know Him, for He lives with you and will be in you (John 14:16-17).

But the Counselor, the Holy Spirit, whom the Father will send in My name, will teach you all things and will remind you of everything I have said to you (John 14:26).

But when He, the Spirit of truth, comes, He will guide you into all truth. He will not speak on His own; He will speak only what He hears, and He will tell you what is yet to come. He will bring glory to Me by taking from what is Mine and making it known to you (John 16:13-14).

Because the Master Gardener always carries out the will of the King, His presence in us enables us to do the same. In this way, under His guidance, we can shape our lives and behavior into beautiful gardens that accurately reflect the heart, nature, and character of our King.

One way the Holy Spirit enacts God's will and brings this about in our lives is by asserting God's authority in the world, especially against the pretender and his agents. That's what a governor does. He establishes the authority of his king in the new territory. Many people, both inside and outside the Kingdom, are confused about who the Holy Spirit is and what He does. Some see Him only as the most mysterious Person of the Godhead, the Trinity, about whom little is known or can be known. To others, He is the one who sends tingles down people's spines and gives them "warm fuzzies" during worship, the one who knocks people down and rolls them around on the floor. Those things may happen sometimes, but they do not reflect the environment or atmosphere of Heaven, nor do they reflect the reason the Governor came.

Heaven is a place of peace, harmony, and order, because it is the home of the King. The Holy Spirit is not some divine joy-buzzer or stun gun to give believers a jolt; He is a Person whose job is to mold them into the likeness of the King.

Once, when I was conducting some meetings in Venezuela, a young man came to me and asked if I could help his brother. He told me quietly that his brother had "problems with spirits." I told him I would be glad to help. After the meeting, he took me behind the curtain near the steps where I saw a young man looking up at me with a tortured expression on his face. He was very dirty, and when I approached him, he blew his top. He fell on the ground and started screaming.

I knew that the Governor lived in me and that this man was God's property. Picking the man up, I told the spirit to shut up, and the young man immediately fell quiet. I said to the spirit, "You know this is the end of your possession," and the spirit cried out, "I know!" Then I said, "Leave now."

The young man fell to the ground again and rolled over. I could actually smell the evil spirit as it departed. Afterward, this young man's brother helped him to his feet, and he grabbed me and started crying. I told his brother to get him something to eat, because evil spirits literally starve the body.

At the next session the following morning, this young man was sitting on the front row with his brother, weeping from joy and worshiping the Lord. No stress, no strain, no spiritual gymnastics or pyrotechnics; just the peace and joy of one who has been restored to his place in his Father's Kingdom, free once more to manifest his Father's culture. A new garden was blooming. The Governor is here to bring back the culture of Heaven.

THE HOLY SPIRIT MEDIATES GOD'S PRESENCE

As Governor, the Holy Spirit mediates for the people of Earth on behalf of the absent King. Although the dominion of God the Father covers both Heaven and Earth, He maintains His presence in Heaven; and in this aspect of His divinity, He has not come down to the Earth. He has, however, come to Earth in the Persons of His Son, Jesus Christ, and the Holy Spirit. The New Testament tells us that the Son of God took on human flesh, announced the arrival of the Kingdom of Heaven, and then died by crucifixion, shedding His sinless blood so that we sinners could gain access to the Kingdom. Forty days after His resurrection from the dead, Christ ascended to Heaven, where He is now seated at the right hand of His Father and where He continues to intercede on our behalf. Ten days after He ascended, He sent the Holy Spirit to live permanently in the hearts of believers so that there would always be a presence of God on the Earth.

Even though the king and queen of England rarely visited the Bahamas during our colonial days, we were always conscious of their presence because the governor who resided in that imposing pink house on Duke Street was the king and queen personified. They might be absent in body, but in the person of the governor their authority was ever-present.

Every year the governor called us together for an official meeting. The whole community gathered in a big park by the beach for the annual "Day of the Reading of the Speech from the Throne." A red ceremonial chair would be set out with a crown behind it, and the governor would sit in the chair and read to us the words of the king or the queen. The governor never told us anything that the king or queen did not write. He never spoke to us on his own authority, but only on the authority delegated to him by the government.

It is the same way with the Holy Spirit. As we saw earlier, Jesus said in John 16:13 that the Holy Spirit will never speak on His own but will speak only what He hears. And what the Spirit does say will always be in agreement with what the Father and the Son say and with what the Bible, the written Word of God, says. None of these will ever contradict any of the others; they will always be in perfect accord.

As Governor of the Kingdom, the Holy Spirit is the official, designated representative through whom all information from and about the King and His Kingdom passes to His citizens. Because He is in Heaven, seated at the right hand of His Father, it is impossible for us to receive any information from Christ, our King, except through the Holy Spirit. The Spirit is the one who guides us into all truth (see John 16:13), teaches us all things, and reminds us of everything Jesus taught us (see John 14:26). As long as the Governor is here, the

King is here. As long as the Governor is here, the presence, power, and authority of the King are here. As long as the Governor is here, the Kingdom of Heaven is present on the Earth.

The Holy Spirit is the presence of the absent King. Jesus Christ is in Heaven, seated at His Father's right hand. His work on Earth is finished. But He promised not to leave His followers as orphans (see John 14:18), so He asked His Father to send "another Counselor" to be with them forever (see John 14:16). In Greek, the word for "another" means another of the same kind. The Spirit who was to come would be exactly like Jesus except that He would actually be present in believers rather than just *with* them, as Jesus was. The Greek word for "Counselor" is *parakletos*, which literally means "one called alongside" as a helper. This perfectly describes the Holy Spirit's role as Governor of the Kingdom and His ministry as Teacher, Guide, and Master Gardener: to nurture and bring fully to life gardens of truth in the lives of believers.

The Governor of the Kingdom mediates the presence of the King. So wherever the Governor is present, the King is present, and so is His Kingdom. And since the Governor resides in our hearts as Kingdom citizens, we take the King and the Kingdom wherever we go. One distinct characteristic of the Kingdom is that wherever it passes, it leaves in its wake life, restoration, and transformation.

The desert shall rejoice and blossom as the rose. . . . Waters shall burst forth in
the wilderness, and streams in the desert. The parched ground shall become a
pool, and the thirsty land springs of water (Isaiah 35:1b; 6b-7a NKJV).

This is God's big idea, His strategy for filling the Earth with gardens of His Kingdom.

CONNECTING TWO WORLDS

Living inside every Kingdom citizen and believer in the Lord Jesus Christ is the most powerful Person on Earth, yet most of us don't realize it. Oh, we are quick to say, "Yes, I believe the Holy Spirit is in me," or, "I know I have been baptized in the Spirit," but few of us are truly conscious of the magnitude of the Person and power of the Holy Spirit. We don't know Him, we don't listen to Him, and, depending on our background, we may even have been taught not to expect much from Him. Instead, we would much rather watch television or talk to our friends or spend our time following the enticements of the world. However, if we want to grow as Kingdom citizens and reach our fullest potential in fulfilling our mission to plant Kingdom gardens throughout the world, we must take time to get to know the Master Gardener. We must learn to listen to Him and obey.

Why? For one thing, He is our link between Heaven and Earth, and in Him we are connected to both worlds. The Holy Spirit is the bridge between the supernatural and the natural realms. We say that God rules a "supernatural" Kingdom, but this is strictly a human perspective. The word *supernatural* does not occur in the Bible, and for a very simple reason: From God's perspective, which is also the Bible's perspective, the concept is meaningless. For that matter, we would be more correct to speak of the spiritual domain as a *supranatural* realm. The prefix *supra* means "outside" or "above." Heaven is a supranatural realm because it is above and outside our own, but to God there is no distinction. Natural and supranatural are the same to Him because He created both realms. The only difference is that one is lower than the other.

Jesus moved between the natural and the supranatural with ease, and so does the Holy Spirit. Furthermore, because the Holy Spirit dwells within us, He enables us to transcend the boundary between the two, so that our prayers and praise and worship can rise to Heaven, and God's presence, power, and privilege (favor) can flow down to us. In this way, we can reproduce the character and culture of His Kingdom on Earth. It is like being able to cross international borders with no checkpoints, customs, or passports. The Holy Spirit is our passport; through Him we have access to anywhere in the Kingdom, including the throne room of the King Himself. I don't know about you, but that's the way I want to live...and it is the way I am learning how to live.

When Jesus told Pilate, *"My kingdom is not of this world"* (see John 18:36), He was acknowledging two things: first, that He was the King of a real Kingdom, and second, that His Kingdom was from another place, a place outside and above the physical realm. A kingdom, remember, is the governing influence of a king over his territory or his domain, impacting it with his will, purpose, and intent; and that is manifested in the culture, lifestyle, and quality of life of his citizens. So in acknowledging His Kingship to Pilate, Jesus was telling the Roman governor that He had a country with a society of citizens and a moral code, and that it possessed territory, power, and influence—yet it was not from Earth.

At the same time, however, His Kingdom was in place *on* the Earth. Citizens of His supranatural realm lived as immigrants in the natural realm but maintained their allegiance to their parent country, Heaven. They were in the world but not of the world.

This characterization describes all of us who are Kingdom citizens. We are a distinct society within the greater society of humanity in general. We are a counterculture to the popular culture. Our loyalty is to our heavenly King. If it comes down to a choice between obeying the local government or the heavenly government, the heavenly government wins out every time. Even though we are in the world, we live under a different government and are obliged to do and say only that which is consistent with that government.

Jesus said that He did nothing on His own but only what He saw His Father doing (see John 5:19,30). He spoke only what His Father told Him to speak (see John 8:28). As Kingdom citizens, we have the same responsibility. By connecting us to our home world while we remain in this one, the Holy Spirit enables us to hear and understand the words and will of our King and empowers us to carry them out. That is a nice way to live. It means we never have to argue. All we have to do is obey. If someone questions our words or behavior, all we have to do is say, "I'm operating under the laws of my government." It is our Governor's responsibility and joy to take that which comes from the head, or top—the King's will and desires—and make sure that it reaches all the way to the bottom and out to the citizens, who bring it to fruition in the world around them.

FROM TOP TO BOTTOM

All of our talk about reproducing Kingdom gardens on Earth is simply another way of saying that God is in the process of re-colonizing the planet with His Kingdom government and culture. This mission was so critical that He could entrust it to no one other than His Son, who alone possessed all the necessary qualifications. Jesus came into the world as a government agent on special assignment. Pilate, too, was a government official. This is why he understood Jesus' words, whereas the religious leaders did not; he and Jesus were talking kingdom language.

The word "colony" comes from the Latin word *colonia*, which is transliterated into the Greek as *kolonia*. Colony comes from the word *colere*, which literally means "cultivate," as in planting and nurturing a garden. To colonize, therefore, (or to plant Kingdom gardens) means to cultivate a people in one place to be just like a kingdom in another place. It means to reproduce a culture. In fact, the word *culture* itself comes from the Latin *cultura*, which also means "cultivation." The word *agriculture* (from *ager*, Latin for "field" or "land") is the art of cultivating the soil to produce crops. Similarly, *horticulture* (from *hortus*, Latin for "garden") is the art of growing fruits, vegetables, flowers, or ornamental plants. So the Holy Spirit truly is the Master Gardener, because His purpose is to cultivate Kingdom government and culture in the hearts of Kingdom people, and through them, to reproduce more of the same all over the world until the Earth is filled with them.

A root word for colony and colonization is *colon*, which is also the name given to the human digestive tract. Although we think of the colon most often as the large intestine, the word actually encompasses the entire system, beginning with the tongue and esophagus, through the stomach, small intestine, and large intestine, all the way to the rectum. How does this connect with colonies and cultivation of gardens? It is a Greek concept. Your colon begins in your head and ends in your bottom. Whatever goes into your head and is consumed will end up in the bottom, guaranteed. If you doubt it, take a teaspoonful of some good Jamaica pepper (allspice) and wait several hours—it will make a believer out of you!

Here is the connection the Greeks made. They said that the key to government is to get what is in the head out to the bottom of the community. The king is the head, and he appoints a governor to communicate and establish his will and desires throughout the community at the bottom (the colony). Similarly, the job of a master gardener is to execute the will and desires of the garden owner (the head) and produce a garden (the bottom) that satisfies those desires. This is the role of the Holy Spirit in our lives, to ensure that we as Kingdom citizens reproduce the character and culture, and live according to the values, standards, and principles of our King. It is this top-to-bottom process that Jesus had in mind when He taught His disciples to pray, *"Your kingdom come, Your will be done on earth as it is in heaven"* (Matt. 6:10).

When this connection is made from top to bottom, from Heaven to Earth, from the King to His citizens through the link of the Holy Spirit, the result will be a manifestation of Kingdom power and authority that is as attractive as it is undeniable. There is no better example of this than the life of Jesus. By His own declaration, Jesus did nothing on His own, but only what He saw His Father doing (see John 5:19). And what did Jesus do? He healed the sick, made the lame to walk, gave sight to the blind, hearing to the deaf, and speech to the mute. He cast out demons and raised the dead. Jesus did all these things because He saw them first in the mind and heart of His Father. He knew these things were His Father's will, so He did them. The "colon" was clear. The border between countries was open, and the loving, merciful, compassionate, and healing will of the King passed from His supranatural realm into the realm of the natural.

Jesus is in Heaven now with His Father, but His Spirit, His Governor, His Master Gardener, is here in His stead, and He wants to do the same things in and through us that Jesus did. God's will and purposes never change. Jesus Christ is the same yesterday, today, and forever (see Heb. 13:8). He gave us this promise:

I tell you the truth, anyone who has faith in Me will do what I have been doing. He will do even greater things than these, because I am going to the Father (John 14:12).

The Holy Spirit came to dwell in us for the purpose of fulfilling this promise in and through us. Christ is the Head, in Heaven, and we are His Body, on Earth. The Governor delivers the will of the Head to the Earth and carries it out through us, the Body. The Master Gardener takes the seeds and plans of the Owner and transfers the Garden of His supranatural realm into the natural world.

Chapter Five

WHO TENDS YOUR GARDEN?

O N the face of it, God's Garden Expansion Program for reproducing His Kingdom culture in our lives sounds so simple. The King expresses His will to the Governor, and the Governor brings it to fruition in the lives of His citizens. What could be easier? And yet for so many believers, the process breaks down somewhere along the way. Countless citizens of the Kingdom neither live according to Kingdom government consistently nor manifest Kingdom culture convincingly. Why not? Because they take no care as to whose garden grows in their lives. Sometimes they do not even know who tends their garden.

Successful gardens may have many caretakers, but only one master gardener, one person whose vision oversees the overall design. More than one guiding plan leads to confusion, inefficiency, inconsistent results, and stunted fruitfulness. This is precisely the dilemma many believers face. On the one hand, they claim to follow the King and to live according to His government, while on the other, they continue to listen to the desires of the pretender and fail or refuse to uproot the "weeds" of evil, rebellion, and destruction he has sown in their hearts. And then they wonder why their garden is choked off and produces little fruit.

Gardens are known by the consistency, quality, and abundance of the fruit they produce; and these are direct reflections of the skill and character of the gardener. Jesus expressed it this way:

No good tree bears bad fruit, nor does a bad tree bear good fruit. Each tree is recognized by its own fruit. People do not pick figs from thornbushes, or grapes from briers. The good man brings good things out of the good stored up in his heart, and the evil man brings evil things out of the evil stored up in his heart. For out of the overflow of his heart his mouth speaks. Why do you call Me, "Lord, Lord," and do not do what I say? (Luke 6:43-46)

The quality of the fruit depends on the nature of the root. In other words, the fruit we bear in our lives reveals who is tending our garden. There are only two choices: either the Holy Spirit, the Master Gardener, is in control, or else the pretender runs the show. And the fruit they produce could not be more different. Writing to the Galatian believers, the apostle Paul captured perfectly this contrast, as well as the dilemma faced by believers who try to balance between two gardeners:

So I say, live by the Spirit, and you will not gratify the desires of the sinful nature. For the sinful nature desires what is contrary to the Spirit, and the Spirit what is contrary to the sinful nature. They are in conflict with each other, so that you do not do what you want. But if you are led by the Spirit, you are not under law. The acts of the sinful nature are obvious: sexual immorality, impurity and debauchery; idolatry and witchcraft; hatred, discord, jealousy, fits of rage, selfish ambition, dissensions, factions and envy; drunkenness, orgies, and the like. I warn you, as I did before, that those who live like this will not inherit the kingdom of God. But the fruit of the Spirit is love, joy, peace, patience, kindness, goodness, faithfulness, gentleness and self-control. Against such things there is no law. Those who belong to Christ Jesus have crucified the sinful nature with its passions and desires. Since we live by the Spirit, let us keep in step with the Spirit. Let us not become conceited, provoking and envying each other (Galatians 5:16-26).

Every day we all make choices that determine which fruit will manifest in our lives: either the bad fruit of the pretender or the good fruit of the Master Gardener. Satan illegally stole the throne of the earthly dominion that rightly belonged to man and turned that domain into a spiritual wasteland. And since the natural reflects the supernatural, we see, in the many ways that the human race has mistreated the planet and misused its resources, a representation of the spiritual devastation wrought by the pretender's depraved rule.

The Bible is the record of God's plan to reclaim the earthly dominion and restore it to His original design and intent. As we have already seen, God's big idea from the beginning was to extend His heavenly Kingdom to Earth, and He chose to do it through His very own children. This was not a religious act but an act of state. Adam and Eve had no religion in the Garden of Eden. What they did have was continuing fellowship with their Creator as they ruled the created order as His vice-regents. In bringing Heaven to Earth, the King was simply enacting His own governmental policy. His purpose was to fill the Earth with His glory. He wanted to bring His own nature to the Earth, and that nature was reflected in the lush beauty, abundant fruitfulness, and absolute perfection of the Garden.

SEEKING AND SAVING WHAT WAS LOST

It was not God's purpose, however, to leave Heaven and come to Earth to rule it directly. He chose instead to give rulership of this domain to beings specially created for it. God created human beings specifically for the purpose of dominating the Earth for Him and filling it with His nature, character, and culture. No other created beings in Heaven or on Earth were suited for the task. Only humans were fit to rule the Earth because that is the way God designed us. First He created the territory, and then He created the kings to rule it. He said, "The earth is ready; now I will release the children, and they will dominate the land in My name."

Unfortunately, in an act of treason and betrayal, the first two humans inadvertently surrendered their kingdom to one who greatly desired it but who was not qualified to rule it. Satan, also known as lucifer, had originally been part of the angelic host (spiritual beings created as servants of the King). Angels were not created to rule but to do the King's bidding. Lucifer rebelled, however, along with one-third of the angels of Heaven. Cast out of Heaven, he set his sights on gaining control of the earthly realm, dominating not only it, but also the human vice-regents God had placed over it. In this he succeeded. A demonic pretender ascended the throne, and the earthly realm declared its independence from Heaven.

Jesus Christ, the King's Son, came to Earth to take it back. He came to regain what was lost. When Jesus announced the arrival of the Kingdom of Heaven in Matthew 4:17, He was not bringing anything new to the Earth. He was bringing back what man had lost and what the pretender had stolen.

One day Jesus and His disciples were passing through the city of Jericho and stopped at the home of a man named Zacchaeus, a tax collector. Although a Jew, Zacchaeus was despised by his own people, who saw him as a traitor for collaborating with the hated Roman occupation government. Furthermore, Zacchaeus cheated the people by charging more tax than the Romans demanded and enriching himself by pocketing the difference.

When Jesus entered the tax collector's house, He brought the Kingdom with Him, and Zacchaeus found it irresistible. His encounter with the King and the Kingdom changed Zacchaeus forever.

> But Zacchaeus stood up and said to the Lord, "Look, Lord! Here and now I give half my possessions to the poor, and if I have cheated anybody out of anything, I will pay back four times the amount."
>
> Jesus said to him, "Today salvation has come to this house, because this man, too, is a son of Abraham. For the Son of Man came to seek and to save what was lost" (Luke 19:8-10).

Notice that Jesus said He came "to seek and to save **what** was lost," rather than "who" was lost. Other versions of the Bible translate the phrase, "that which was lost." Certainly, in context, Jesus was referring to Zacchaeus, who found salvation the day he encountered the Kingdom of Heaven. Until that day, Zacchaeus had been allowing the wrong person to tend his garden and had the bad fruit in his life to prove it. The moment he encountered Jesus and the Kingdom of

Heaven, however, he turned everything over to the Master Gardener and immediately began to bear good fruit. Another Kingdom garden had been planted.

But Jesus was referring also to the Kingdom of Heaven itself, which had been lost, and which He came to seek and to save. In fact, the word *save* here literally means "to salvage, to restore what was lost," not just to restore people to their status as children of God in relationship with Him, but also to restore to them the dominion lost by their ancestors, Adam and Eve. People everywhere are looking desperately for the Kingdom, even if they don't know it. This is why, when they encounter it—when they hear the message of the Kingdom—they, like Zacchaeus, find it irresistible. It is this attractive, magnetic quality of the Kingdom that Jesus had in mind when He said, *"From the days of John the Baptist until now, the kingdom of heaven has been forcefully advancing, and forceful men lay hold of it"* (Matt. 11:12). Once people know about the Kingdom and understand it, they flock to it, desperate to enter. This is only natural. The Kingdom is what we were created for.

IT'S TIME TO CHANGE OUR THINKING

When Adam and Eve declared independence in the Garden by disobeying God's one restriction, they thought they could govern themselves and their earthly domain at least as well as God could, if not better. They were wrong. No sooner had they "freed" themselves from God's control than they found themselves deposed from their earthly thrones altogether. Their sin against God corrupted their human nature, and they became enslaved to the power and will of the pretender. He preferred to work behind the scenes, however, pulling the strings while letting them think they were governing themselves.

Humanity's efforts at self-government have been disastrous from the beginning. As we have already seen, the first act of human self-government after leaving Eden was an act of fratricide: Cain murdered his brother Abel. As a race, we humans have been chained by envy, hatred, and murder ever since. Thousands of wars and six millennia of social, scientific, and technological advancement have not changed things to any great degree. Our world is just as hate-filled and as violent as ever. Despite all our proud claims of advancement and bettering ourselves, we are actually getting worse. Rather than bringing about self-improvement, all our efforts at self-government have moved us closer and closer to self-destruction.

The King who created us loved us too much to let us destroy ourselves, so He sent His Son to the Earth to restore His Kingdom and bring His wayward, rebellious human children back under His government. Jesus Christ inaugurated His public mission by announcing the return of the Kingdom and calling people to respond: *"Repent, for the kingdom of heaven is near"* (Matt. 4:17b). To *repent* means to change your mind; it involves a radical readjustment of one's thinking. Jesus was saying, in effect, "OK, everybody, the true Kingdom, the Kingdom of Heaven, has arrived. It's time to change the way you've been thinking, because the one who has influenced you to think that way is wrong. Everything the pretender has told you is wrong. He is a liar and the father of lies."

When Christ came to the Earth, He brought the Governor, the Holy Spirit, with Him, but the Governor could not be released to His full work until Christ completed His assignment and returned to Heaven. For 33 years, from Jesus' birth to His ascension, the Holy Spirit showed up nowhere on the Earth except in Jesus Himself. Because of sin, no humans were adequate vessels in which the Holy Spirit could dwell. We had to be cleaned up first. This is why Jesus came, and why He could not stay.

Christ came to announce the return of the Kingdom and to give us access to it through His death, by the cleansing of our sins with His blood. His resurrection from the dead guaranteed eternal life to all who place their faith in Him. Then, by ascending to Heaven and returning to His Father, He enabled the releasing of the Holy Spirit to take up permanent residence in the life of every believer. The Governor returned to His mansion; the Master Gardener was back on the grounds.

Jesus Christ preached the Gospel of the Kingdom, which was His primary reason for coming. But His Kingdom message would mean nothing unless the sin that separated all people from God was removed. The Governor could not inhabit a sin-soiled vessel. So Jesus completed His mission by dying on a cross, shedding His sinless blood to save, or salvage us and restore us to a right relationship with our heavenly Father.

The Gospel, or "good news," is not only the blood of Jesus, but also the message of the Kingdom of Heaven—that it has arrived and is available for all to enter. The blood of Jesus is the cleansing agent that we must pass through in order to make our "house" clean so that the Governor can take up residence. The death of Christ on the cross was absolutely necessary because "[God's] *law requires that nearly everything be cleansed with blood, and without the shedding of blood there is no forgiveness*" (Heb. 9:22).

The Bible says that all of us have sinned and fallen short of God's righteous standard (see Rom. 3:23). Sin is rebellion against God, which separated us from Him and made the "houses" of our lives dirty and unholy, unfit for the presence of a holy Governor. The sinless blood of Jesus has the power to thoroughly cleanse our house and make it holy again.

After Jesus rose from the dead, one of His first acts was to appear to His disciples and release the Holy Spirit to be with them forever:

> *On the evening of that first day of the week, when the disciples were together, with the doors locked for fear of the Jews, Jesus came and stood among them and said, "Peace be with you!"*
>
> *After He said this, He showed them His hands and side. The disciples were overjoyed when they saw the Lord.*
>
> *Again Jesus said, "Peace be with you! As the Father has sent Me, I am sending you." And with that He breathed on them and said, "Receive the Holy Spirit. If you forgive anyone his sins, they are forgiven; if you do not forgive them, they are not forgiven"* (John 20:19-23).

Christ the King came to Earth, took His property back from the pretender who had stolen it, and then returned to Heaven, leaving the Governor in charge. Jesus likened this aspect of His mission to overpowering a strong man:

*No one can enter a strong man's house and carry off his possessions unless he
first ties up the strong man. Then he can rob his house* (**Mark 3:27**).

The "house," or the earthly dominion, was originally given to us, the human
race. We lost it to satan, the "strong man." The Owner came to Earth to get His
house back and return it to His children. Then, to ensure that His children need
never again fall into satan's bondage, He shed His blood to cleanse their sins and
set them free forever. The cross broke the power of the devil over the lives of
everyone who repents of their sins and turns in faith to Christ for their cleansing. Anyone who lives under satan's control lives under an illegal government.

We need to stop allowing the wrong person to tend our garden. It is time to
change both our thinking and our behavior to bring them in line with who we
really are. Christ set us free. Through His death and resurrection, He cleansed
us of our sin—our rebellion against God—and gave us access to His Kingdom.
Then He gave us the Governor to teach us how to live as Kingdom citizens. The
Governor, the Holy Spirit, is the Master Gardener who ensures that the gardens
of our lives produce good fruit that is appropriate and pleasing to the King, to
whom the gardens belong. Could there be any greater freedom—or any greater
destiny—than this?

No Fear of the Devil

This question of who tends our garden is vitally important, because whoever tends the garden controls the fruit. Whoever tends our garden determines
our culture, our values, our beliefs, and our behavior. God created us. He fashioned our bodies from the dust of the ground and breathed His life into us. We
belong to Him; we are His house. The devil wants to take up residence in us
through demonic powers because he knows that once he is inside he can work
through us to wield his evil influence at home, at school, at work, at church, in
the neighborhood, in the community, and even in the nation.

We were created to be filled with the Spirit of God and to live in perfect
harmony and fellowship with Him, not to be under the thumb of a demonic

pretender exercising illegitimate authority. This is why, whenever Jesus encountered a demonic spirit possessing a human being, He cast out the spirit on the grounds of illegal residence. As believers, we have a choice as to whom we allow to tend our garden. One choice leads to a wasted and unfulfilled life, while the other leads to great abundance and fullness of life. The apostle Paul described the choice this way:

> *In the same way, count yourselves dead to sin but alive to God in Christ Jesus. Therefore do not let sin reign in your mortal body so that you obey its evil desires. Do not offer the parts of your body to sin, as instruments of wickedness, but rather offer yourselves to God, as those who have been brought from death to life; and offer the parts of your body to Him as instruments of righteousness. For sin shall not be your master, because you are not under law, but under grace. . . . You have been set free from sin and have become slaves to righteousness. . . . But now that you have been set free from sin and have become slaves to God, the benefit you reap leads to holiness, and the result is eternal life. For the wages of sin is death, but the gift of God is eternal life in Christ Jesus our Lord* (Romans 6:11-14,18,22-23).

We have been trained by religion to be scared of the devil. Most of our churches have taught us to regard the world situation as hopeless, to prepare ourselves to leave, and then to pray for the Lord to rescue us out of this world. Having conceded victory to the pretender, we feel that all we can hope to do is to circle the wagons and defend ourselves as best we can until Christ comes back and takes us away. We have become a bunch of holy sissies. Not only is this an unnecessarily pessimistic and defeatist mindset, it also runs contrary to the expressed will and purpose of our King. Consider these words that Christ Himself prayed regarding His followers the night before He was crucified: *"My prayer is not that You take them out of the world but that You protect them from the evil one"* (John 17:15).

Jesus' prayer says nothing about our leaving the world. He doesn't even pray for satan to be removed from the scene. Instead, He asks His Father to *protect* us from the evil one. Ultimately, satan the pretender poses no threat to us. His rule on Earth is illegal; legitimate dominion belongs to us, the children of God, just as He established it in the beginning. In league with our King, we have more power and authority than any fallen angel could ever hope to have. No angel was ever given a dominion to rule. No angel was ever given permission to cast out demons (which are, in fact, fallen angels).

Kingdom citizens, on the other hand, rule the Earth by divine decree and possess global authority to evict demonic spirits. We are not in a servile position toward angels. On the contrary, their job is to serve us. As the writer of the Book of Hebrews asks rhetorically, *"Are not all angels ministering spirits sent to serve those who will inherit salvation?"* (Heb. 1:14). We are the legal rulers on Earth with the power, authority, and protection of our King behind us. Satan is a liar, usurper, and pretender whose illegal power over us was broken forever at the cross. Although we must always be on our guard against his schemes, deception, and treachery, as Kingdom citizens exercising our legitimate authority, we have no reason to fear him.

The devil, however, has every reason to fear us because we have the Governor residing in us. And he does fear us. He understands better than most of us the magnitude of the power and authority that are ours as children of the King and rightful heirs to the Kingdom. Having gone head-to-head against the power of the Kingdom and lost, he knows by bitter experience that ultimately he stands no chance against the legitimate heirs. This is why he seeks to gain advantage over us through lies, trickery, deceit, insinuation, distraction, indirect attacks, and temptations of all kinds. He knows that if he can get us to forget who we are and become convinced that we are powerless against him, he will win. So the next time you sense that the devil is attacking you in some way, remember that he is coming at you from a position of weakness, not strength, and from a posture of fear, not confidence. At heart, the devil is a coward. When faced with someone who truly is not afraid of him, he runs away. James states this explicitly: *"Submit yourselves, then, to God. Resist the devil, and he will flee from you"* (James 4:7).

If we are Kingdom citizens and children of God, satan has no authority over us. He can't even touch us without God's permission (see Job 1–2), so what are we afraid of?

STRENGTH IN TRIALS

We are so in the habit of being afraid of the devil that whenever any kind of trial or trouble comes along, we immediately assume it is a demonic attack. We earnestly pray to the Lord to deliver us without ever considering the possibility that the trial may have come for the purpose of strengthening our faith and helping us to grow toward spiritual maturity. James, the brother of the Lord Jesus, wrote:

> *Consider it pure joy, my brothers, whenever you face trials of many kinds, because you know that the testing of your faith develops perseverance. Perseverance must finish its work so that you may be mature and complete, not lacking anything* (James 1:2-4).

Do these sound like the words of someone who fears the enemy or someone who is getting ready to "skip town," expecting to be taken out of the world at any moment? No, these are the words of someone determined to *occupy* until the Lord comes (see Luke 19:13 KJV). For those who do occupy and stand firm, a rich reward lies in store:

> *Blessed is the man who perseveres under trial, because when he has stood the test, he will receive the crown of life that God has promised to those who love Him* (James 1:12).

Temptation is a fact of life in a fallen world. For Kingdom citizens, however, temptation does not have to mean fear or failure, but can be the catalyst for strengthening and growth. Satan tempts with the intent to destroy, but Kingdom citizens have an advantage not available to those outside the Kingdom: the King Himself places a limit on how much temptation He allows us to face. As the apostle Paul wrote to the believers in the city of Corinth:

No temptation has seized you except what is common to man. And God is faithful; He will not let you be tempted beyond what you can bear. But when you are tempted, He will also provide a way out so that you can stand up under it (I Corinthians 10:13).

If our King will not allow us to be tempted beyond what we can bear, that means that whatever temptations we *do* face, we *can* bear, as long as we do so in His strength rather than our own. The Governor is always with us, and His strength is readily available to us, so we need not fear anything the devil tries to do to us. God is committed to the glory of His name, the growth of His Kingdom, and the good of His children. And He will do whatever is necessary to turn everything to serve His divine purpose, even the evil efforts of the enemy. As Paul wrote to the Roman believers:

And we know that in all things God works for the good of those who love Him, who have been called according to His purpose. For those God foreknew He also predestined to be conformed to the likeness of His Son, that He might be the firstborn among many brothers. And those He predestined, He also called; those He called, He also justified; those He justified, He also glorified. What, then, shall we say in response to this? If God is for us, who can be against us? He who did not spare His own Son, but gave Him up for us all—how will He not also, along with Him, graciously give us all things? (Romans 8:28-32)

Our protection from the evil one is certain because of the King's love for us. And because the Governor lives in us, nothing can stand in the way of His love. Again, in the words of Paul:

No, in all these things we are more than conquerors through Him who loved us. For I am convinced that neither death nor life, neither angels nor demons, neither the present nor the future, nor any powers, neither height nor depth, nor anything else in all creation, will be able to separate us from the love of God that is in Christ Jesus our Lord (Romans 8:37-39).

TESTED FOR WEAKNESS

First Corinthians 10:13 says that God will not allow us to be tempted beyond what we can bear. The Greek word for *tempted* literally means "to test for weakness." It is the same word used for the process of testing a sword for strength and proper forging—what we would call *tempering* today. This was done by putting the sword in fire. The steel for the sword was heated until it was red-hot, beaten flat into the proper shape, and then held up to reveal any grayish spots in the red-hot metal that indicated areas of weakness. The sword then went back into the fire, and the weak spots were beaten with a hammer on an anvil to smash the molecules together so they would be tighter and stronger. After this, the sword was placed in cold water in order to freeze the molecules in place. Then it was heated to red-hot again and reexamined for weak spots. This process of examination, hammering, cooling, reheating, and reexamining was repeated until all the weak spots were beaten out of the sword. Only then was the sword ready for use in battle. An untested sword might break in the heat of battle, with deadly consequences for the soldier who used it.

So the word *tempt* means "to test for weakness," not out of a desire to destroy, but for the purpose of making one strong and unbreakable. When the Bible says that God will not allow us to be tempted beyond what we can bear, it means He will not allow the devil to strengthen our weak areas without His permission. Despite satan's evil intent, temptation does not come to destroy us but to strengthen us where we are weak.

Why are we afraid of the devil? Why do so many of us give him free reign to tend our garden his way? He is a defeated enemy with no power or authority over us except what we allow him to have. Satan is no match for God. Even in his rebellion, satan inadvertently ends up serving God's ultimate purpose by strengthening the weaknesses of his own enemies through temptation.

At this point, let me make it perfectly clear that God never tempts anyone to evil. James writes:

When tempted, no one should say, "God is tempting me." For God cannot be tempted by evil, nor does He tempt anyone; but each one is tempted when, by his own evil desire, he is dragged away and enticed. Then, after desire is conceived, it gives birth to sin; and sin, when it is full-grown, gives birth to death. Don't be deceived, my dear brothers. Every good and perfect gift is from above, coming down from the Father of the heavenly lights, who does not change like shifting shadows. He chose to give us birth through the word of truth, that we might be a kind of firstfruits of all He created (James 1:13-18).

Satan tempts us by enticing us in the areas where he knows we are weak. His intent is to distract us, to induce us to turn our hearts away from our King and His righteous government, and to destroy our usefulness as Kingdom citizens. If we, however, rather than turning away and giving in, rely on the strengthening presence of the Master Gardener in our hearts, He can give us the grace to persevere; and in persevering, we grow stronger in the weak area in which we are being tempted. We do not possess the strength to persevere on our own, and the Lord does not expect us to. That is why He gave us the Holy Spirit as a permanent resident in our hearts.

As Kingdom citizens and children of God, we have no reason to fear the devil as long as we are seeking first the Kingdom of God and His righteousness (see Matt. 6:33). The devil fears us because the greatest power in the universe is on our side, and the Creator and King of the universe Himself lives in us through His Spirit. Greater is He who is in us than he who is in the world (see 1 John 4:4). We are more than conquerors through Him who loved us (see Rom. 8:37), and we can do all things through Christ, who gives us strength (see Phil. 4:13). Against such power and invincibility, the devil can't help but be afraid.

LISTEN TO THE MASTER GARDENER

When Jesus inaugurated His public ministry by being baptized in the Jordan River by John the Baptist, the Holy Spirit descended upon Him like a dove (see Matt. 3:16). The first thing the Holy Spirit did was lead Jesus into the wilderness to have His weak areas tested by the devil. After 40 days the test was over, and Jesus passed with flying colors. He emerged from the desert full of the Master Gardener and of power. He called the first of His disciples, and then went into a local synagogue, where he encountered a man possessed by a demonic spirit.

> *Just then a man in their synagogue who was possessed by an evil spirit cried out, "What do You want with us, Jesus of Nazareth? Have You come to destroy us? I know who You are—the Holy One of God!"*

> *"Be quiet!" said Jesus sternly. "Come out of him!" The evil spirit shook the man violently and came out of him with a shriek* (Mark 1:23-26).

Christ's arrival on the earthly scene put the devil on notice. The Kingdom on Earth was being taken from him and restored to its rightful overlords. The devil was being kicked out of the garden, and the Master Gardener was taking over.

Who is tending your garden? Have you given free reign to the illegal pretender to fill your mind with the weeds of his evil thoughts, desires, fears, and imaginations? Or have you yielded the fertile soil of your mind to the skillful and loving hands of the Master Gardener, allowing Him to cultivate in you the rich and abundant fruit of Kingdom government and culture? The way of the pretender leads to futility and death; the way of the Master Gardener leads to fulfillment and life. The choice is yours.

The psalmist draws the contrast quite clearly:

> *Blessed is the man who does not walk in the counsel of the wicked or stand in the way of sinners or sit in the seat of mockers. But his delight is in the law of the Lord, and on His law he meditates day and night. He is like a stream planted by streams of water, which yields its fruit in season and whose leaf does not wither. Whatever he does prospers. Not so the wicked! They are like chaff that the wind blows away. Therefore the wicked will not stand in the judgment, nor sinners in the assembly of the righteous. For the Lord watches*

over the way of the righteous, but the way of the wicked will perish (Psalm 1:1-6).

Listen to the voice of the Master Gardener. Let Him strengthen you in your weak areas so that you can stand firm and become a distinctive Kingdom presence in the world around you. Let Him make of your life a garden truly fit for the King.

Chapter Six

UNDERSTANDING GARDEN INFLUENCE

B Y now it should be abundantly clear that the Kingdom of Heaven is not a religion and has nothing at all to do with religion. In Eden, the original Kingdom Garden on Earth, there was no religion. There was no *worship* in the sense that we usually understand the word. Adam and Eve enjoyed full, open, and transparent fellowship and interaction with their Creator in a mutual relationship of pure love with absolutely no guilt, shame, or fear. Their disobedience broke that relationship, and humanity's efforts to restore it on their own without divine assistance gave rise to religion.

The Kingdom of Heaven is the sovereign rulership of the King (God) over a territory (Earth). He impacts it with His will, purposes, and intent, producing a citizenry of people (*ekklesia*—the Church) who express a culture reflecting the nature and lifestyle of the King. Therefore, as we have seen, the Kingdom of Heaven is a real, literal country, although invisible to physical eyes because it is spiritual in nature. As King of Heaven, God's big idea was to extend the influence of His heavenly country over and throughout the Earth. So we are really talking about two things here: God's country and its influence.

In reading the four Gospels of the New Testament—Matthew, Mark, Luke, and John—it becomes immediately clear that Jesus used two similar but different phrases to refer to the country of the King and the influence of the King. Sometimes He referred to the "Kingdom of Heaven," and at other times to the "Kingdom of God." Although it is common to use these phrases interchangeably, there is an important difference in focus. The phrase "Kingdom of Heaven" refers to the literal place, the "headquarters" country of God. "Kingdom of God," on the other hand, refers to the King's influence wherever it extends, but especially its extension into the earthly realm. Another way to explain the distinction is to say that while we can *go* to the Kingdom of Heaven, we can *bring* the Kingdom of God to the Earth. Heaven is the place; the Kingdom of God is the influence. That is why Jesus said, *"The kingdom of God is within you"* (Luke 17:21b). Wherever the Kingdom of God is, the Kingdom of Heaven has influence. So wherever we go as Kingdom citizens, the influence of the King should go along.

The most powerful expression of any nation is its culture: its values, morals, customs, codes of conduct, standards of living, modes of dress, food, and dietary practices, etc. A strong and rich culture can wield an influence far beyond its geographical boundaries. France is a good example. Historically, French culture has a high and proud heritage with truly worldwide influence, particularly in the areas of language and the culinary arts. Many English words—"croissant" for example—either were borrowed directly from the French or are of French origin or derivation. French cooking is deservedly famous around the world and so influential that even to this day most of the terminology used in Western cooking is French (such as *sauté*). One reason French culture has had such tremendous influence is because Louis XIV, the "Sun King," was the most powerful monarch in European history. The culture of his kingdom spread not only throughout Europe, but also to all nations worldwide that were originally colonized by European nations. So, even though the kingdom of Louis XIV is long gone, the influence of its culture remains.

God is after the same result for His Kingdom culture and influence on the Earth. He wants people all over the world to see the evidence of His Kingdom in the values and lifestyles of His citizens and to be drawn to that influence.

IRRESISTIBLE INFLUENCE

There are two kinds of influence: the influence of the moment, which spreads rapidly and then disappears just as quickly; and lasting influence, which grows more slowly, but succeeds through persistence and permeation. Momentary or fleeting influence includes such fads as fashion, hairstyles, and the latest "popular" books, which are here today and gone tomorrow. These superficial influences, and others like them, may make a big stir in society for a time, but they generally lack the depth and substance to effect any significant changes in the culture. Influence that lasts operates more subtly and works from the inside out, altering external appearances and behavior by changing internal values, beliefs, and mindsets.

Kingdom influence is of the second type. It operates gradually, based on eternal, unchanging principles of God and according to a timetable that encompasses millennia. God literally has all the time in the universe to fulfill His plan. Consider this: at least 4,000 years passed from the time Adam and Eve lost the kingdom in Eden until Christ announced its return. More than 2,000 years have elapsed since Jesus walked the Earth, and God's ultimate plan has still not yet reached completion. But throughout all that time, His influence has been growing and expanding gradually and sometimes almost invisibly, permeating human culture. And none of the efforts of either humans or the pretender can stop it.

Ultimately, the influence of God's Kingdom is irresistible. This does not mean that everyone eventually will enter the Kingdom, but it does mean that someday everyone will acknowledge the reality, authority, and absolute supremacy of the Kingdom of Heaven. The apostle Paul stated plainly that the day will come when:

at the name of Jesus every knee should bow, in heaven and on earth and under the earth, and every tongue confess that Jesus Christ is Lord, to the glory of God the Father (Philippians 2:10-11).

The word *Lord* means "owner" and is a term properly applied to a king. Christ is the King of an eternal, all-powerful, all-knowing, omnipresent Kingdom, and one day everyone will confess that this is so, even those who have rejected His Kingdom.

The subtle yet irresistible nature of the Kingdom was the subject of several of Jesus' parables, or teaching stories:

This is what the kingdom of God is like. A man scatters seed on the ground. Night and day, whether he sleeps or gets up, the seed sprouts and grows, though he does not know how. All by itself the soil produces grain—first the stalk, then the head, then the full kernel in the head. As soon as the grain is ripe, he puts the sickle to it, because the harvest has come (Mark 4:26-29).

As with the mysterious way of seeds in the Earth, the Kingdom of God grows silently and invisibly, until one day, like the harvest-ready grain, the evidence of its presence is there for all to see.

The kingdom of heaven is like a mustard seed, which a man took and planted in his field. Though it is the smallest of all your seeds, yet when it grows, it is the largest of garden plants and becomes a tree, so that the birds of the air come and perch in its branches (Matthew 13:31-32).

The Kingdom of Heaven is so subtle and unassuming in its growth that many people ignore it or dismiss it altogether as completely inconsequential. Eventually, however, it will grow to be revealed to everyone as it really is: the greatest Kingdom of all, next to which the kingdoms of man are nothing.

The kingdom of heaven is like yeast that a woman took and mixed into a large amount of flour until it worked all through the dough (Matthew 13:33).

Anyone who spends any amount of time in the kitchen knows what yeast is and what it does (knowing *how* it does what it does is another matter). Yeast is one of the most powerful influencing agents in the world, and it exists for one reason: to infect whatever it is mixed into with its presence and influence. Jesus' comparison of the Kingdom of Heaven to yeast makes us think right away about impact.

While people caught up in religion think about leaving the Earth, Kingdom citizens focus on transforming it the way yeast transforms a batch of dough. Yeast is not about giving up or giving in. It is about taking over. Yeast does not abandon dough; it affects it. Yeast never becomes dough. Instead, dough becomes what bakers call "yeast dough." Dough is weaker than yeast, and as the yeast works its way through, the dough gradually but irresistibly takes on characteristics created by the yeast.

Yeast has not finished its job until it has "worked all through the dough." In the same way, Christ is not coming back to an Earth that is not "worked all through" with the influence of His Kingdom. He wants our courts, our parliaments, our congresses, our legislatures, and our executive mansions at all levels to be thoroughly overtaken by His government influence. He wants our schools and our workplaces to be totally infected by Kingdom culture. He wants every home, every marriage, and every family to be completely possessed by Kingdom impact. The King is not interested in partial measures; He is coming to take back the entire planet. In fact, Jesus specifically stated, "*This gospel of the kingdom will be preached in the whole world as a testimony to all nations, and then the end will come*" (Matt. 24:14). Kingdom business, therefore, has nothing to do with abandoning Earth. We are in the business of influencing the Earth, of spreading gardens of Kingdom culture and government throughout the world. Christ has promised that if we preach the Gospel of the Kingdom, He will make sure that the whole world hears the message.

PETITIONING THE GOVERNMENT

In previous chapters we have already talked about the Kingdom prayer Jesus taught His disciples to pray, but we need to keep returning to it because it is also His Garden expansion prayer:

> *Our Father in heaven, hallowed be Your name, Your kingdom come, Your will be done on earth as it is in heaven* (Matthew 6:9b-10).

"On earth as it is in heaven": that is our number one prayer. We should not pray for rapture. We should not pray for retreat. We should not pray for rescue. We should pray for *revolution*. Every time we pray for God to take us out of the world, we are praying the wrong prayer. Instead, we should pray for Heaven to come to Earth—for His Garden to spread until it fills the planet.

One of the words for *prayer* in the New Testament also means "petition." A petition is a legal act. It is used to address a government. Often, when we read the word *prayer* in the New Testament, it is talking about petitioning. You only petition government. For many believers, prayer does not work the way it should because they have made it a religious exercise of pleading for a favor rather than a legal act of asserting their rights and privileges as Kingdom citizens. Prayer is business with the government of God. It is where we bring a legal claim to legitimate government authority and demand the government's response.

Becoming a Kingdom citizen through faith in Christ and through the cleansing of our sins by His blood gives us complete access to all the rights, resources, and privileges of the Kingdom. When we petition the King properly (in the right spirit of humility and in accordance with His will), we are only asking for what He has already promised. This is why, even in humility, we can ask with boldness and confidence, which is what the writer of the Book of Hebrews had in mind when he wrote,

> *Let us then approach the throne of grace with confidence, so that we may receive mercy and find grace to help us in our time of need* (Hebrews 4:16).

Jesus' prayer shows us not only what we should ask for, but also the manner in which we should petition the government. First, He says we must address our petition to the right Person: "*Our Father in heaven.*" God the Father is the King who is ruling in Heaven, and we are His citizens in His Garden outpost on Earth who are petitioning for an audience.

Second, we must pay proper respect when addressing the King: "*hallowed be Your name.*" To hallow God's name means to render utmost respect and reverence to His name, because His name is identified with His reputation. And because God is very jealous of His reputation, He is also jealous of His name. This is why He commanded the Israelites, "*You shall not misuse the name of the Lord your God, for the Lord will not hold anyone guiltless who misuses His name*" (Exod. 20:7). This goes far beyond merely using God's name as a curse word. It also includes such things as misrepresenting Him before others and claiming openly to be a believer while living like the devil. To hallow God's name means to fear Him with a holy fear, to be so overwhelmed by Him that we constantly acknowledge the awesomeness of His power and want to make sure that He never thinks we take Him for granted. Why do you hallow the King? Because He holds the power of life and death. When we petition the government, we must first show proper respect to the government.

Third, our petition should always reflect not our own will, but the will of the King, for the will of the King is law: "*Your kingdom come, Your will be done on earth as it is in heaven.*" Remember, this is Jesus instructing His disciples how to pray. In other words, the King Himself is telling us what to ask Him for. He says nothing about cars or clothes or food. Instead, He says, "Petition for My government influence to come to Earth, for My intentions, purposes, culture, lifestyle, and will to be done on Earth just as they are in Heaven."

PRAYING FOR YEAST

When we focus our hearts and minds to pray for Heaven to come to Earth, then the next part of Jesus' Garden-expansion prayer makes more sense: "*Give us today our daily bread*" (Matt. 6:11).

The meaning should be clear: When we tend to God's business, He will tend to ours. This connection between praying for Heaven to come to Earth and receiving our daily bread ties in directly to what Jesus says a few verses later: *"But seek first* [God's] *kingdom and* [God's] *righteousness, and all these things will be given to you as well"* (Matt. 6:33).

"All these things" refers to our everyday needs. *"Daily bread"* certainly refers to food, but it is also much more than that. The ancient Jews often used the word *bread* as an idiom that meant everything necessary for life. In essence, Jesus was saying, "If you pray for My government to come to Earth in your job, in your business, in your home, in your community, in your government, in your schools—in every arena of life—I will meet every need you have."

This promised provision of daily bread can be linked to yeast and its influence. As we pray for God's Kingdom to come, He gives us daily bread—the yeast of His influence—to help us bring about His Kingdom expansion on Earth.

If you are one of those people who have trouble praying because you never know what to pray for, I have just destroyed your last excuse. You don't have to pray long as long as you pray right. Take the time every day—at your bedside when you first get up, while in the shower, while getting dressed, while driving to work, or whatever—to pray simply, "Lord, let Your Kingdom come and let Your will be done in my life today as it is in Heaven." Start praying that prayer, and look for opportunities that God gives you for fulfilling it. Tend to God's business this way, and watch how He starts tending to yours.

Even Jesus' prayer for His followers in John chapter 17 is a "yeast" prayer:

> *My prayer is not that You take them out of the world but that You protect them from the evil one. They are not of the world, even as I am not of it. Sanctify them by the truth; Your word is truth. As You sent Me into the world, I have sent them into the world* (John 17:15-18).

Just as yeast is not of the dough but comes from outside and infects it, so Kingdom citizens are not of the world but of a Kingdom from outside the world, and they infect the world with that Kingdom's culture. In effect, Jesus was praying, "Father, don't take My 'yeast' out of the dough. Protect them from the evil one so that they will be free to permeate the dough thoroughly."

Whatever business, profession, or career you are in, you are the King's yeast wherever you are, and if you set your heart and your prayers right, He will prosper you. But you must have the right attitude. Rather than saying, "I am in business for myself for my own profit," learn to say, "I am in His business for His influence."

Jesus prayed that we not be taken out of the world system. He wants us right in the middle of it: the economic system, the political system, the cultural system, the social system, the entertainment system, the sports system, the investment system, and the health system. We cannot "yeast" the dough if we are not in the dough.

Many believers say, "I want a Christian job with a Christian boss in a Christian workplace." While there certainly are believers whom the Lord has called to such positions, He calls most of us to bloom and prosper right where we are, in the middle of the finance field, the hotel field, the food industry, education, or government, because there is a whole lot of dough out there with a whole lot of needs. He wants us to infect the hospitality industry, banking, business, politics, sports. We are not here to escape; we are here to reshape. Our prayer should be, "Lord, prosper me, not for my sake but for Yours, so I can infect my world with Your Kingdom. Let me be yeast for You." If you pray that kind of prayer, and truly mean it, God will prosper your work.

MAGNETIC ATTRACTION

One of the reasons for the significant power of the Garden influence is its unmistakable appeal. The Kingdom message draws people like a magnet. Even people who have no idea of what they are looking for, or if they are even looking for anything, the moment they hear about the Kingdom they say, "That's it!"

Most people intuitively recognize true and priceless value when they see it. Jesus emphasized the supreme value of the Kingdom in two brief parables:

> *The kingdom of heaven is like treasure hidden in a field. When a man found it, he hid it again, and then in his joy went and sold all he had and bought that field. Again, the kingdom of heaven is like a merchant looking for fine pearls. When he found one of great value, he went away and sold everything he had and bought it* (Matthew 13:44-46).

These parables speak of two different types of people and their responses to the Kingdom. The man in the first parable is like most of the people in the world, either searching aimlessly for something they don't know or simply going through life unaware of the priceless treasure at their feet until they stumble upon it (seemingly) by accident. This man may have heard a rumor of treasure in the field and gone looking for it, or he may simply have been crossing the field and came upon the treasure unexpectedly. Either way, the moment he found it, he knew it was what he had been seeking all his life. He immediately recognized its priceless value and that it was worth any price he had to pay to obtain it. Accordingly, he sold everything he had and bought the field. The Kingdom of Heaven is far more valuable than anything this world has to offer.

In the second parable, the merchant knew what he was looking for: fine pearls. Finding one of "great value," he knew right away that in beauty and worth, it far outstripped any other pearl he had ever found, and he too sold everything he had in order to buy it.

Many people know they are searching for something, for some sense of meaning and purpose to life, and some even have at least a vague idea of what they want. They sample different religions, try out various philosophies, and comb through the world's wisdom literature looking for answers and searching for truth. Upon discovering the Kingdom (or being discovered by it), they know intuitively that here, finally, is the answer to all their questions and the end of their long quest.

No matter who we are or where we are from, the Kingdom of Heaven is the only thing we are truly searching for and the only thing we truly need, because the Kingdom gives us access to all the riches of Heaven and all the resources of eternity.

The appeal of the Kingdom of Heaven is so magnetic, in fact, that it draws in people of every nation, culture, and language group, including many who, although attracted to the obvious benefits of Kingdom life, never understand the principles behind it or reach the place of true faith to embrace it. These, as in Jesus' parable of the wheat and the weeds, will in time be separated out from true Kingdom citizens. The King's invitation is wide open, of truly global scope, but not everyone will accept it. As Jesus made clear, many are called, but few are chosen.

> *Once again, the kingdom of heaven is like a net that was let down into the lake and caught all kinds of fish. When it was full, the fishermen pulled it up on the shore. Then they sat down and collected the good fish in baskets, but threw the bad away. This is how it will be at the end of the age. The angels will come and separate the wicked from the righteous and throw them into the fiery furnace, where there will be weeping and gnashing of teeth* (Matthew 13:47-50).

As with the wheat and weeds that grow together until the harvest, good "fish" and bad "fish" will mingle together in the "sea" of the world until the day when the Kingdom of Heaven draws them all in with its all-encompassing net. Then all who have responded to the King's invitation will be welcomed into the fullness of Kingdom life, while those who have not will be separated out forever.

Jesus told another parable with a similar point, but one which also reveals more of the abundance that awaits those who accept the King's invitation:

> *The kingdom of heaven is like a king who prepared a wedding banquet for his son. He sent his servants to those who had been invited to the banquet to tell them to come, but they refused to come.*

Then he sent some more servants and said, "Tell those who have been invited that I have prepared my dinner: My oxen and fattened cattle have been butchered, and everything is ready. Come to the wedding banquet."

But they paid no attention and went off—one to his field, another to his business. The rest seized his servants, mistreated them and killed them.

The king was enraged. He sent his army and destroyed those murderers and burned their city. Then he said to his servants, "The wedding banquet is ready, but those I invited did not deserve to come. Go to the street corners and invite to the banquet anyone you find."

So the servants went out into the streets and gathered all the people they could find, both good and bad, and the wedding hall was filled with guests. But when the king came in to see the guests, he noticed a man there who was not wearing wedding clothes.

"Friend," he asked, "how did you get in here without wedding clothes?"

The man was speechless.

Then the king told the attendants, "Tie him hand and foot, and throw him outside into the darkness, where there will be weeping and gnashing of teeth."

For many are invited, but few are chosen (Matthew 22:2-14).

Entrance into the Kingdom of Heaven is open to all, for the King excludes no one from His invitation. Jesus said,

If anyone is thirsty, let him come to Me and drink. Whoever believes in Me, as the Scripture has said, streams of living water will flow from within him (John 7:37b-38).

He also promised, *"To him who is thirsty I will give to drink without cost from the spring of the water of life"* (Rev. 21:6b). The invigorating waters of Kingdom life are offered to all without cost or exclusion, yet many will exclude themselves by refusing to drink.

The drawing power of the Kingdom is so great and so all-encompassing that ultimately no one will be able to resist its attraction. Everyone will be drawn: either to liberation and life for those who believe, or to judgment and death for those who do not. Either way, no one will escape the magnetic attraction of the Kingdom of Heaven—or the just judgments of its righteous and holy King.

KINGDOM COMMUNITY AND CULTURE STOPPED

The ultimate power and goal of Garden influence is to develop a heavenly culture on Earth that produces a Kingdom community. God wants to invade Earth with Heaven, to infuse Earth with Heaven's culture until Earth begins to look just like Heaven. His desire is to build a heavenly community on Earth through the cultivation of His Kingdom culture here. This is exemplified both in the prayer of Jesus: *"Your kingdom come, Your will be done on earth as it is in heaven"* (Matt. 6:10), and in the plan of God from the beginning: *"Let Us make man in Our image…and let them rule…"* (Gen. 1:26).

God doesn't want a religion. He doesn't want a weekend ceremony. He isn't looking for a group of weird people dressed in weird clothes saying weird things. God wants a holy community of whole and complete citizens, a community that represents and reflects Heaven on Earth, and He wants to do it through cultivating His Kingdom's culture on Earth through the lives and influence of His people.

Chapter Seven

CREATING A
KINGDOM CULTURE

GOD'S big idea has three simple goals: to reclaim the Earth for the King-dom of Heaven, create a Kingdom culture on the Earth, and, as a result, produce a Kingdom community throughout the Earth. As I said in Chapter One, all kingdoms seek to expand, usually through either outright conquest or colonization. In the beginning, God established a colony of Heaven on the Earth and placed the first two humans, Adam and Eve, in charge of it. His intent was that they and their descendants would rule the Earth according to His standards and principles and be fruitful and multiply until the entire planet was filled with His people manifesting His glory.

Unfortunately, Adam and Eve proved unwilling to live under God's supreme rule and declared their independence by doing the one thing He told them not to: They ate of the fruit from the tree in the center of the Garden. In other words, Adam and Eve rebelled against their King. However, their experiment in independence and self-rule was a disastrous and utter failure. Human history has demonstrated time and time again that as a race we are manifestly incapable of governing ourselves effectively apart from the Spirit and principles of God. God, of course, knew this from the start, which is why, in the wake of man's rebellion, He set into motion His plan to reclaim, or recolonize, the planet, a plan He established even before the foundations of the Earth were laid. (See Proverbs 8:22-31; Revelation 13:8.)

Recolonization is an unfamiliar concept because it is extremely rare for a colony, once it has declared its independence from a kingdom, to later change its mind and desire to return to colonial status. God, however, initiated the recolonization of Earth for two reasons: because His sovereign will and intent will never be thwarted, and because our survival as a race depends on it.

You will recall that a kingdom is the governing authority of a king over his territory—he impacts it with his will, purpose, and intent, producing a citizenry who reflect the king's morals, values, and lifestyle. In this respect, a kingdom is completely opposite of a republic. In a republic, no one is required to act or think exactly like the president or to take on the president's nature or values. Citizens of a true kingdom, however, are required to take on the king's personal values, morals, and nature. Kingdom citizens are expected to exhibit the lifestyle and culture of the king.

This is why living in a kingdom is much more challenging than living in a democracy. In a democracy your individuality is protected. You can safeguard it. You can be yourself and make it a point of pride. In a kingdom, there is only one "self" to be, and that is the king. Anyone who does not take on the king's nature, his moral standards, or his personal values is regarded as a rebel. Remember that in a kingdom the king's word and will are law, and anyone who challenges that authority is guilty of rebellion against the government.

REVERSING ADAM'S FAILURE

In the Bible, rebellion against God is called sin. This is exactly what Adam and Eve were guilty of in the Garden of Eden. Their deliberate defiance of God's prohibition against eating the fruit of the tree in the center of the Garden was an act of open rebellion. In so doing they were exercising their free will, the freedom to choose that God had given them. Before free will can truly exist, there must also be a component of choice, because free will is only possible where there is an alternative. So the tree in the center of the Garden, and God's prohibition against eating its fruit, provided Adam and Eve with the capacity to use a gift that God had given them. Unfortunately, they used it in the wrong way; they *could* freely have chosen to obey God rather than disobey.

Adam and Eve declared rebellion against the government of Heaven, and the Bible calls it sin. In fact, the Bible speaks in some instances of *sin*, singular, and in others, of *sins*, plural, and there is a difference. *Sin* is the singular act of rebellion, while *sins* are the manifestations of that one act. Rebelling against the Kingdom is sin; sins are the day-to-day actions that constitute rebel-like behavior. The declaration of independence of the Adamic race from the Kingdom of God was an act of rebellion that has caused all of us, like Adam, to go our own way.

This personal independence is the number one tenet of capitalism and democratic republics. The thing God hates is the very thing we magnify. The thing that God says is our condemnation is the very thing we regard as our highest achievement. As independent individuals we can do whatever we like and pursue our own happiness and joy at our own expense. We take great pride in "doing our own thing"; whereas God says, "That's the very problem with the world." It's a paradox. This is why it is very difficult to live in the Kingdom of God and live at the same time in a democracy under a capitalistic system. It is hard to strike a balance between the two, because the principles by which they operate are diametrically opposed to each other. It is for this reason that many believers do not manifest Kingdom culture and values in their lives the way they should. In their struggle between the Kingdom and the world, the world usually wins.

Jesus Christ came to Earth to put an end to our sin of rebellion, and, through His blood, to cleanse us of our sins, the rebellious behavior that was the inevitable consequence of our sin. Christ came as a "second Adam" to reverse the consequences of the first Adam's failure. The apostle Paul explained it this way:

Sin entered the world through one man, and death through sin, and in this way death came to all men, because all sinned. . . . Consequently, just as the result of one trespass was condemnation for all men, so also the result of one act of righteousness was justification that brings life for all men. For just as through the disobedience of the one man the many were made sinners, so also through the obedience of the one man the many will be made righteous (Romans 5:12,18-19).

For as in Adam all die, so in Christ all will be made alive (I Corinthians 15:22).

So it is written: "The first man Adam became a living being"; the last Adam, a life-giving spirit (I Corinthians 15:45).

Christ came to announce the return of the Kingdom of Heaven and to give us access through the sin-cleansing power of His blood. But He also, through His Spirit, placed in us the capacity to manifest Kingdom culture and values in our everyday life so that, as we go about our daily affairs, we can transform our little corner of the world into a thriving garden of His Kingdom.

KNOWN BY OUR CULTURE

Isaiah 45:18 says that God formed the Earth to be inhabited. He planted citizens of His heavenly country here as immigrants on Earth, so they could turn it into a conclave of Heaven. We are the immigrants. We live on the Earth but are not from the Earth. You and I were sent here by our Father out of His own womb. He made us as spiritual beings like Himself, then clothed us in an "earth suit" made from the dust of the ground, to fit us for inhabiting this physical world. We live here but we are not from here. Our homeland is Heaven, and as immigrants, our lives here, both individually and collectively, should reflect unmistakably the culture of our homeland.

Our culture as Kingdom citizens should be just as distinct and obvious as that of San Francisco's Chinatown. The inhabitants of Chinatown live in the United States, and may even be American citizens, but everything about them—their language, their dress, their food, their customs—shows that their origin is from another place. Walk into Chinatown, and suddenly you can't find a hot dog anywhere. Nobody is speaking English. These things are foreign to their culture. Chinatown is not an official "town," but a community created by a group of people who share a common and distinct culture. It is not necessary to travel halfway around the world to learn what life is like in China. All you have to do is visit Chinatown, and you will "see" China, because it is a "garden" of the Chinese homeland that has bloomed in the West.

In the same way, people should be able to walk into our presence or our homes or our churches and feel like they have walked into another country. They should be able to tell immediately by our language, dress, manners, attitude, and behavior that we are not of this world. Our culture should stand out so clearly that no one can mistake it.

Life with Jesus was always this way, which is why He attracted so much attention. People either loved Him or hated Him, accepted Him or rejected Him, but no one ignored Him. Everywhere He went He brought Kingdom culture. Throngs of people surrounded Him because He showed them the power, quality, nature, and irresistible appeal of a culture that could make them victors in life rather than victims—and then He told them how to get it.

One of the biggest struggles Jesus' disciples faced was learning how to shift their thinking and their behavior from the worldly culture of their birth to the Kingdom culture they had entered when they answered Jesus' call to follow Him. Every day He challenged their behavior, beliefs, values, thoughts, perceptions, assumptions, and expectations. They had to learn, for example, that what the world calls a "miracle" is everyday activity in the Kingdom of Heaven.

After the death of His cousin, John the Baptist, Jesus

withdrew by boat privately to a solitary place. Hearing of this, the crowds followed Him on foot from the towns. When Jesus landed and saw a large crowd, He had compassion on them and healed their sick.

As evening approached, the disciples came to Him and said, "This is a remote place, and it's already getting late. Send the crowds away, so they can go to the villages and buy themselves some food."

Jesus replied, "They do not need to go away. You give them something to eat."

"We have here only five loaves of bread and two fish," they answered.

"Bring them here to Me," He said. And He directed the people to sit down on the grass. Taking the five loaves and the two fish and looking up to heaven, He gave thanks and broke the loaves. Then He gave them to the disciples, and the disciples gave them to the people. They all ate and were satisfied, and the disciples picked up twelve basketfuls of broken pieces that were left over. The number of those who ate was about five thousand men, besides women and children (Matthew 14:13-21).

Culture reflects government. In the world's culture, some people go hungry. Some people are poor or sick or lacking some of the basic necessities for a high quality of life. Inequities abound, and injustice is rampant. Not in Kingdom culture. Wherever Jesus went, sick people were made well—because there is no sickness in the Kingdom. Hungry people were fed and satisfied—because there is no hunger or lack of any kind in the Kingdom.

When 5,000 people in a remote place needed to be fed, Jesus did the natural thing (from the Kingdom perspective)—He fed them. His disciples wanted to send the people away to buy food because they were approaching the situation from a point of view of lack. Jesus, however, knew there was no lack because He had unlimited access to the unlimited resources of His Father's Kingdom.

When Jesus took those five loaves and two fish from His disciples, He took them out of an agrarian and fishing economy subsumed under Rome—and into Kingdom-ism. Once inside that new economy, the very atoms in that fish and bread began to behave differently. They began to split and reproduce. Nuclear scientists know that once you split one atom, every other atom can split itself. It is called multiplication. Jesus performed the first atomic act with bread and fish, because in the Kingdom you can actually hand out atoms. What we call a miracle was simply normal activity in the Kingdom. And it should be normal activity for all who manifest Kingdom culture.

As Kingdom citizens, we should be known by our culture, and that culture should change the lives of everyone around us. Sickness, poverty, lack, hunger, fear, discouragement, defeat, curses, greed, lust, envy, jealousy, hatred, violence—none of these exist where Kingdom living prevails. The reason is simple: Kingdom culture reflects the life and environment of Heaven. None of those things are found in Heaven, so they should not be found in Heaven's culture on Earth. Is it any wonder, then, why people in the world would be irresistibly attracted to a community that manifests such a culture?

MANIFESTATIONS OF CULTURE

The ultimate goal of God's Garden Expansion Program is to reproduce on Earth the culture of His heavenly Kingdom—its fundamental principles as well as its language, lifestyle, values, and morals—with the end result of producing an earthly community that looks and acts like Heaven. Culture is the way of life that a people grow into. It is also defined as the conditions under which or within which living things grow. Culture is the inherent lifestyle manifested in the behavior of a distinct people. Again, Chinatown is a prime example. It may exist physically in America, but its culture is distinctly Chinese. The culture of Chinatown is a manifestation of the original homeland of the people who live and work there.

In addition, culture is the total life of a people passed on to their descendants. Culture is an extremely powerful thing. Its roots grow deep, and its influence reaches far. This is why a group of people bound together by culture can live for generations in a country not their own and still maintain their distinct identity. Culture encompasses the totality of life: dress, food, drink, customs, manners, etiquette, protocol, attitudes toward children and the elderly, religious beliefs, ethical and moral values, social norms, and both public and private behavior.

If we are manifesting Kingdom culture in our lives, people who meet us should be able to say, "I think I just entered Heaven. You don't lie, you don't cheat, you don't steal, you don't sleep around, you've been married to the same person for 30 years; what's up with you? Where are you from? Why are you so different?" When people outside the Kingdom look at Kingdom citizens or a Kingdom community, they should see a culture distinctly different—and much more attractive—than their own.

But exactly how does culture manifest? Culture reveals itself in at least 16 specific ways. Let's take a look.

I. VALUES

Every culture manifests itself in values. Values can be defined simply as those things that a society regards as valuable and worth protecting, preserving, and passing on. For example, if a society values divorce, there will be many divorces. In the Kingdom of Heaven, however, divorce is not a value, so it is not supposed to occur. In much of Western society, gay rights and same-sex marriage are fast approaching the status of values and may, before long, enjoy the full protection of the law. These things carry no value in the Kingdom of Heaven, however, because they go against our King's standards.

Some churches and denominational groups have started lowering their standard of values in order to attract more people. Surrendering to political correctness and social pressures, they are adjusting their theology and their doctrine to accommodate personal perversion and give it dignity. The Bible says that those who do such things have no inheritance in the Kingdom of God. In contrast, the Kingdom of God never lowers its standards of value to accommodate anyone's personal preferences. Instead, it challenges people to adjust their preferences to come into alignment with the Kingdom's standards. In effect, the King has said, "Here are the standards for life in My Kingdom. Compliance is mandatory; otherwise, you don't come in."

The Kingdom of Heaven is not some fly-by-night religion. It is a serious government with serious power. The King will not put up with those who claim to live in His Kingdom yet refuse to obey His laws. He will not tolerate rebellion in the ranks. In ancient Israel, the sin of one person was enough to bring God's judgment upon the entire community, and the entire community had to come together as one to remove the offender from their society. When a man named Achan took some of the spoils from the destruction of Jericho for himself in violation of God's command, God withdrew His protection, and the Israelites were defeated in their next battle. It was only after Achan was exposed and confessed his sin, and after the community stoned him to death along with his family, that God's preserving presence and power returned to Israel. (See Joshua 7.)

When the church in Corinth tolerated sexual immorality within its ranks, the apostle Paul minced no words:

> *It is actually reported that there is sexual immorality among you, and of a kind that does not occur even among pagans: A man has his father's wife. And you are proud! Shouldn't you rather have been filled with grief and have put out of your fellowship the man who did this?... I have written you in my letter not to associate with sexually immoral people—not at all meaning the people of this world who are immoral, or the greedy and swindlers and idolaters. In that case you would have to leave this world. But now I am writing you that you must not associate with anyone who calls himself a brother but is sexually immoral or greedy, an idolater or a slanderer, a drunkard or a swindler. With such a man do not even eat. What business is it of mine to judge those outside the church? Are you not to judge those inside? God will judge those outside. "Expel the wicked man from among you"* (I Corinthians 5:1-2,9-13).

Kingdom culture manifests in godly values that are never surrendered, compromised, or watered down at any time for any reason under any circumstances.

2. PRIORITIES

Culture reveals itself also in the life priorities of those who live in the culture. In Western society, for example, priority is given to making money and acquiring wealth and possessions. Capitalism and consumerism are the gods of greed, as many people consume their lives pursuing the almighty dollar (or pound or franc or peso). Yet Jesus said:

> No one can serve two masters. Either he will hate the one and love the other, or he will be devoted to the one and despise the other. You cannot serve both God and Money (Matthew 6:24).

He then went on to describe the priorities of His Kingdom and its culture:

> So do not worry, saying, "What shall we eat?" or "What shall we drink?" or "What shall we wear?" For the pagans run after all these things, and your heavenly Father knows that you need them. But seek first His kingdom and His righteousness, and all these things will be given to you as well. Therefore do not worry about tomorrow, for tomorrow will worry about itself. Each day has enough trouble of its own (Matthew 6:31-34).

In Kingdom culture, the King's priorities are the citizen's priorities. Like Jesus, who said, "I do only what I see My Father doing," Kingdom citizens have no priorities of their own, but only those given to them by the King. He has promised that if we give priority to His Kingdom and His righteousness, He will give priority to our needs.

3. BEHAVIORS

All of us reveal our culture by our behavior. The respect (or lack of respect) that we show toward parents, teachers, law enforcement, and other authority figures speaks volumes about our culture. So do the degree and tolerance level given to such behaviors as public drunkenness, gambling, carousing, lewdness, and the like. Outward behavior gives expression to the content of the heart. Unhealthy behavior is always a sign of an unhealthy culture.

Kingdom behavior is defined by commands such as:

Honor your father and your mother... (Exodus 20:12a).

Children, obey your parents in the Lord, for this is right (Ephesians 6:1).

Do not let any unwholesome talk come out of your mouths, but only what is helpful for building others up according to their needs, that it may benefit those who listen. And do not grieve the Holy Spirit of God, with whom you were sealed for the day of redemption. Get rid of all bitterness, rage and anger, brawling and slander, along with every form of malice. Be kind and compassionate to one another, forgiving each other, just as in Christ God forgave you (Ephesians 4:29-32).

Sober, wholesome, upright, disciplined, and responsible behavior seems to be a vanishing commodity in our increasingly "anything goes" society, but such behavior is the expected norm in the culture of the Kingdom.

4. STANDARDS

Every culture has standards of conduct that determine how people treat one another. Worldly culture as a whole operates by a standard that is essentially selfish, putting one's own welfare ahead of all others. Many people concentrate on grabbing for their own piece of the pie, using and discarding other people in their scramble for the top. It's dog-eat-dog and every man for himself.

Not in the Kingdom of Heaven. The Kingdom operates by a completely different, even opposite standard, which Jesus demonstrated in both word and example. The night before He was crucified, Jesus shared a final Passover meal with His disciples. Before the meal, He took off His outer clothing, wrapped a towel around His waist like a servant, and proceeded to wash the dirty, smelly feet of His disciples. This was a task normally relegated to the lowest of slaves. Afterward, He explained what He had done:

> *When He had finished washing their feet, He put on His clothes and returned to His place. "Do you understand what I have done for you?" He asked them. "You call Me 'Teacher' and 'Lord,' and rightly so, for that is what I am. Now that I, your Lord and Teacher, have washed your feet, you also should wash one another's feet. I have set you an example that you should do as I have done for you. I tell you the truth, no servant is greater than his master, nor is a messenger greater than the one who sent him. Now that you know these things, you will be blessed if you do them"*
> (John 13:12-17).

On another occasion, when the disciples were arguing about which of them was the greatest, Jesus set them straight:

> *Sitting down, Jesus called the Twelve and said, "If anyone wants to be first, he must be the very last, and the servant of all"* (Mark 9:35).

The standard of conduct for greatness in the Kingdom of Heaven is not self-promotion but servanthood.

5. CELEBRATIONS

Another distinguishing feature of a culture is found in the celebrations it observes. Whatever we celebrate, we elevate. In other words, we show what is most important to us by the things we give special attention to. I repeat: Whatever we celebrate, we elevate. Whatever we elevate, we worship. Whatever we ignore, we destroy. If your nation, state, or community celebrates "Gay Pride Day" every year with a parade, it says a lot about your culture. If you celebrate annually the anniversary of the legalization of abortion, it says a lot about your culture.

God gave the ancient Israelites seven festivals to celebrate throughout the year in commemoration of events such as His deliverance of them from slavery in Egypt (Passover), and His care, preservation, and provision for them in the wilderness (Feast of Tabernacles). Kingdom culture celebrates significant events in the life of God's people. We celebrate Christmas in commemoration of the birth of our Lord and Savior Jesus Christ, and Easter in remembrance of His resurrection from the dead. In our worship communities we regularly celebrate Communion, or the Lord's Supper, in memory of how Jesus' body was broken and His blood shed on the cross for the cleansing of our sins and to give us access to His Kingdom.

6. MORALITY

One of the clearest indicators of the nature and health of a culture is the moral climate it encourages. For example, a society that winks at or ignores prostitution, adultery, pornography, homosexual behavior, cohabitation, out-of-wedlock pregnancies, and abortion is a society on the road to destruction.

All of these things are diametrically opposed to the moral standards of the Kingdom of Heaven. Kingdom culture says:

> *You shall not murder. You shall not commit adultery. You shall not steal. You shall not give false testimony against your neighbor. You shall not covet your neighbor's house. You shall not covet your neighbor's wife, or his manservant or maidservant, his ox or donkey, or anything that belongs to your neighbor* (Exodus 20:13-17).

Kingdom culture also says:

> *But among you there must not be even a hint of sexual immorality, or of any kind of impurity, or of greed, because these are improper for God's holy people. Nor should there be obscenity, foolish talk or coarse joking, which are out of place, but rather thanksgiving. For of this you can be sure: No immoral, impure or greedy person—such a man is an idolater—has any inheritance in the kingdom of Christ and of God* (Ephesians 5:3-5).

When Kingdom citizens live according to these moral standards, they will stand out to such a degree that the world cannot help but take notice.

7. RELATIONSHIPS

People reveal their culture by their relationships: who and what they relate to as a nation, as well as the nature and character of their personal and interpersonal relationships. In the arena of international politics, for example, a nation reveals its culture by who it makes alliances with and why. A country that aligns itself with a terrorist state or repressive regime reveals that it has a culture sympathetic to terrorism, or at least a culture that places trade agreements and economic benefits above human rights, dignity, and worth.

Interpersonal relationships in a worldly culture often are characterized by superficiality and self-centeredness, with people looking out for their personal interests first and valuing other people only as commodities for filling emotional, sexual, or professional needs.

Kingdom culture always puts others ahead of self and puts love over all. When asked to identify the greatest commandment of all, Jesus said:

> *"Love the Lord your God with all your heart and with all your soul and with all your mind." This is the first and greatest commandment. And the second is like it: "Love your neighbor as yourself." All the Law and the Prophets hang on these two commandments* (Matthew 22:37-40).

Unconditional, unselfish love is the single greatest distinguishing factor of Kingdom culture. As Jesus instructed His disciples:

> *A new command I give you: Love one another. As I have loved you, so you must love one another. By this all men will know that you are My disciples, if you love one another* (John 13:34-35).

And the apostle Paul adds this counsel:

Do nothing out of selfish ambition or vain conceit, but in humility consider others better than yourselves. Each of you should look not only to your own interests, but also to the interests of others (Philippians 2:3-4).

These Kingdom principles of love, humility, and selfless regard for others apply to every human relationship without exception or limitation.

8. ETHICS

The character of a nation's culture also is revealed in the ethical standards it practices. These may be quite different from the "official" standards established by law for ethical behavior. Many corrupt and unethical governments have given lip service to the highest ethical standards, even as their leaders victimized the people and plundered the treasury for their own enrichment. Corruption as the moral fabric of a culture guarantees the poverty of a nation, not only economically, but morally and spiritually as well.

On a more personal level, actions such as padding the books, failure to deliver what was promised, and taking advantage of people's ignorance or inexperience by charging them more for goods or services because you know they will never know the difference—all of these are unethical practices symptomatic of worldly culture; they have no place in the life or behavior of a Kingdom citizen.

Kingdom culture means treating everyone with fairness, equality, dignity, and worth. It means doing an honest day's work for an honest day's pay. It means not taking unfair advantage of someone even when the opportunity arises. It means being honest in all of one's dealings and being true to one's word, even to personal detriment.

9. SOCIAL NORMS

Social norms are behaviors that a society accepts as normal; and they are reliable revealers of culture. In the Bahamas, for example, many people accept the practice of "sweethearting" as a normal activity. "Sweethearting" means that a husband or wife has another lover, or "sweetheart," on the side. Americans call it "having an affair," but whatever terminology is used, we are still talking about infidelity—adultery. Calling it an "affair" or "sweethearting" dresses it up and makes the whole thing sound more like a great romantic adventure than the terrible affront and sin that it is, both to God and to one's spouse. Any society that accepts unholy behavior as social norms will be an unholy society and will manifest an unholy culture.

What are the social norms for the Kingdom of Heaven? For one thing, Kingdom culture says, "Be faithful to your spouse." The apostle Paul provides a good list of others:

> *Make sure that nobody pays back wrong for wrong, but always try to be kind to each other and to everyone else. Be joyful always; pray continually; give thanks in all circumstances, for this is God's will for you in Christ Jesus. Do not put out the Spirit's fire; do not treat prophecies with contempt. Test everything. Hold onto the good. Avoid every kind of evil* (I Thessalonians 5:15-22).

10. ATTITUDES

Culture reveals itself also in the attitude of the people. There are certain countries you can visit where the people are very warm and friendly, are appreciative of visitors, and go out of their way to make them feel welcome. I love visiting places like that. At the other end of the spectrum are those countries where the people in general are rude, arrogant, or superior in their demeanor, where even people in the "service" industries, such as hotels and restaurants, act as though they are insulted by your presence and they are doing you a favor by serving you.

No one should ever feel unwelcome when they enter a place where Kingdom culture is present. On the contrary, they should feel as though they have entered Heaven itself. This is why the Bible says, "Let love prevail among you." That is the culture of Heaven. "Let forgiveness prevail among you." That is the culture of Heaven. "Let joy unspeakable prevail among you." That is the culture of Heaven. "Let the peace that passes understanding prevail among you." That is the culture of Heaven.

11. Dress

Another distinctive feature of cultural identity is dress or style of dress. Many people reveal their culture by the kind or cut of clothing they wear. In contemporary Western society it has become commonplace for people, especially young women, to dress in a sexually provocative manner, parading around in public wearing clothes that emphasize—and often barely cover—their breasts and genitalia. This is regarded as acceptable by an increasing number of people in society, including growing numbers of believers who claim to be living as Kingdom citizens. "Everybody does it," they say, or, "That's just the way it is."

To those folks I say, "Well, you're not 'everybody.' They are from another culture; you are from the Kingdom of Heaven, and Kingdom culture says, 'Dress modestly. Dress according to the way you want to be addressed; the way you want to be treated. If you want to be respected, dress respectfully. If you want to be taken seriously, dress accordingly.'" This applies to men as much as to women. If you want to advance in your career or profession, dress for the job you want, not the job you have.

An old proverb says, "Clothes make the man (or woman)." As Kingdom citizens and royal children, we represent our heavenly Father, the King. We should always dress in a manner that honors Him and accurately reflects our status as members of the royal family.

12. Food

Distinctive cultures have distinctive foods. In the Bahamas we have peas and rice and conch salad. America has hot dogs and barbecue. What food distinguishes Kingdom culture? The "food" of the will and Word of God. Jesus said, "*My food. . . is to do the will of Him who sent Me and to finish His work*" (John 4:34). He also said, "*Blessed are those who hunger and thirst for righteousness, for they will be filled*" (Matt. 5:6). The psalmist says that the "blessed" man is one whose "*delight is in the law of the Lord, and on His law he meditates day and night*" (Ps. 1:2). Like a healthy, fruitful tree, such a person will prosper in everything he does. Kingdom culture is characterized by a love and a hunger for the Word of God, and Kingdom citizens feast on its riches.

13. RESPONSE

Culture is revealed in the way people respond to each other, particularly to provocation or mistreatment. The world says, "You hit me; I'll hit you back. Slap me, and I'll slug you. Wound me, and I'll kill you. Betray me, and I will get my revenge."

Kingdom culture is completely different. We do not have to respond in kind to provocation or mistreatment, because our King Himself defends His people. As Paul reminds us:

> Do not take revenge, my friends, but leave room for God's wrath, for it is written, "It is Mine to avenge, I will repay," says the Lord. On the contrary: "If your enemy is hungry, feed him; if he is thirsty, give him something to drink. In doing this you will heap burning coals on his head." Do not be overcome by evil, but overcome evil with good (Romans 12:19-21).

Jesus made it very clear that responding in love no matter how we are treated marks us as citizens of the Kingdom:

> You have heard that it was said, "Eye for eye, and tooth for tooth." But I tell you, Do not resist an evil person. If someone strikes you on the right cheek, turn to him the other also. And if someone wants to sue you and take your tunic, let him have your cloak as well. If someone forces you to go one mile, go with him two miles. Give to the one who asks you, and do not turn away from

the one who wants to borrow from you. You have heard that it was said, "Love your neighbor and hate your enemy." But I tell you: Love your enemies and pray for those who persecute you, that you may be sons of your Father in heaven (Matthew 5:38-45a).

Response is a *choice*, even when responding to provocation or mistreatment, and Kingdom culture always chooses to respond in love.

14. Drink

As with food, culture reveals itself by what people drink. For example, beer drinking is part of German culture, just as it is in Ireland. In the Bahamas we drink tea every day, a holdover from our British colonial days. Kingdom culture thrives on drinking the "living water" of Christ, as He spoke of one day to a Samaritan woman at Jacob's well outside the village of Sychar:

"If you knew the gift of God and who it is who asks you for a drink, you would have asked Him and He would have given you living water."

"Sir," the woman said, "You have nothing to draw with and the well is deep. Where can You get this living water?"...

Jesus answered, "Everyone who drinks this water will be thirsty again, but whoever drinks the water I give him will never thirst. Indeed, the water I give him will become in him a spring of water welling up to eternal life" (John 4:10-11,13-14).

15. Whatever Is Permitted

Culture manifests in what the people permit. We reveal much about ourselves by what we are willing to tolerate. Years ago I visited Amsterdam in the Netherlands, and the host pastor deliberately drove me through the city's "red-light district" so I could see firsthand some of the challenges that he and other Kingdom leaders in that country faced. As soon as we hit the area, I immediately sensed demonic powers in the air. We passed blocks and blocks of storefronts with completely naked women advertising their "wares." People can walk along and "shop" for the one they want, and it is all entirely legal. No wonder that country is a cesspool of immorality.

What we permit reveals our culture. As Kingdom citizens we are not on this Earth to permit immorality, depravity, and corruption. We are here to plant a new culture, the King's culture, a culture of holiness, righteousness, and justice. We are here to reproduce "gardens" of the Kingdom of Heaven wherever we are and to fill the Earth with the fragrance of His presence and glory. We are here to transform the culture of the world by bringing the values, morals, and standards of God's Kingdom and culture to bear in our neighborhoods, communities, and nations.

16. WHATEVER IS ACCEPTED

Finally, culture is revealed by what the people are willing to accept. Permitting something is one thing, but accepting it is another. Acceptance develops from permission. Once something has been permitted long enough, it becomes familiar enough that people no longer question it or resist it. It has become accepted. This is why Kingdom citizens must be always alert and absolutely uncompromising when it comes to Kingdom culture and standards. All it takes is one small concession, one tiny step of compromise, to begin sliding down the slippery slope to immorality, corruption, and destruction. For this reason, we must be careful and faithful to heed the Bible's counsel to stand firm.

FROM CULTURE TO COMMUNITY

The ultimate goal of creating Kingdom culture is to produce a Kingdom community—a community of citizens who look and act just like they do in the home country. When the Bahamas was still under British colonial rule, we were called the Royal Community. Everything we did had to be just like the queen or the king. Even our land was called Royal Crown Land. Everything was royal. The whole community belonged to the kingdom.

Community means essentially that individuality is gone and everybody lives and works for the good of everybody else. Western society, with its emphasis on independence and individualism, has largely lost touch with the concept of community, and this has affected many churches and believers. The time has come for Kingdom citizens to rediscover and reclaim community as an essential part of Kingdom life. This is critical to the successful reproduction of Kingdom gardens throughout the Earth. After all, a Kingdom community *is* a Kingdom garden.

Chapter Eight

PRODUCING A
KINGDOM COMMUNITY

I HAVE a dream that before I die I will see and be part of a dynamic, growing community of people among whom there is no sickness, no poverty, and no want. Everyone will be debt-free. Depression, worry, and despair will be unknown; every marriage will be strong, successful, and happy; and all the children will respect their parents and live completely free of fear. The entire community will worship the Lord in perfect unity and harmony and with a single common vision.

People from outside will be amazed at what they see. "Do you mean that out of these 50,000 people, nobody is divorced? Why not?"

"Because in our community we don't believe in that. We believe in fixing things up, in repenting, reconciling, and forgiving. That's our nature, our culture."

"Do you mean to tell me that among these 200,000 people there is no incest, no fathers sleeping with their daughters? How can this be?"

"Because in our community such a thing is detestable. We love our children. They are made in God's image, and we care for and protect them. That's our culture."

"Do you mean to tell me that out of half a million people, nobody tells lies?"

"It's true. Lying is unheard of in our community. Truth is our currency. In our community, truth is not the best policy—it is the *only* policy."

I dream of the day when this will be reality. Fantasy, you say? Utopia? No, simply Kingdom culture in action.

It is just this kind of community that everyone on Earth secretly longs for. And it is this longing that fuels so many people's desires to leave this world, because they have heard that Heaven is this kind of community. Most of us carry this dream around with us every day. We dream of Heaven because we can't find the community we want here on Earth. You can't wait to get to Heaven because you just got divorced and you hurt so much. You want to go to a place where the hurt is gone. You long for Heaven because your husband just beat you again, and you want to escape to a place where you are always safe. You cry out for Heaven because your uncle molested you for years when you were a child, and now the guilt and shame are so great that you want to go someplace where these things don't happen and where you can be healed. You pray for Heaven because life on Earth is hell.

Jesus says, gently and lovingly, "That's the wrong prayer. Don't pray to go to Heaven; pray for Heaven to come down. Pray, 'Father, let Your Kingdom come and Your will be done on Earth as it is in Heaven.'" He wants Heaven to happen here. We don't have to die to experience Heaven. Jesus said, "Ask for it, and I'll give it to you, here and now."

The possibility of Heaven on Earth is a difficult concept for most of us to grasp because we have been so thoroughly indoctrinated into the culture of this world, where lying is normal, stealing is a habit, adultery is accepted, and sweethearting is still a norm. We have to break that old mindset and be cultured all over again into the heart and mind of God and into the mindset of a Kingdom community.

God's purpose has always been to build a heavenly community on Earth, a community that would reflect in the physical realm the values, principles, standards, morals, and holy and righteous character of His Kingdom in the spiritual realm. The word *community* comes from the words "common" and "unity" and refers to a group of people who share a common language, food, dress, lifestyle, customs, values, and morals. God wants to build His people into a heavenly community on Earth that so reflects Him that anyone from outside who meets us will know immediately that we are not of this Earth. We are in the world but not of the world.

Our assignment as Kingdom citizens and ambassadors is to learn and then to teach others how to apply the Kingdom to business and bodily health; to single life, marriage, and parenting; to investments and speech; to relationships and professions; to government and media. We have to reintroduce the precepts of the Kingdom of Heaven: the values, morals, principles, and standards by which our society is supposed to live. God's plan, then, is not—and never has been—to establish a religious institution, but to build a living, breathing, and thriving community that reveals to the world what He is like as well as the quality of life under His government.

Reflected Glory

The purpose behind a Kingdom community is to reflect the greatness and glory of the King. Citizens of the community are under the rule of the King and come to manifest His nature. In other words, the people take on the characteristics of the King, display the qualities of the King, and exhibit the culture of the King. As a matter of fact, the quality and nature of any kingdom can be recognized first not by the presence of the king but by the lifestyle of his citizens. Seeing how the people in a kingdom live reveals a great deal about their king.

That's how kingdoms work. Kingdoms are manifested in the culture of the people. So the quality of the community is a manifestation or reflection of the quality of the king. This truth is taught throughout Scripture, but no more clearly perhaps than in the account of the queen of Sheba's visit to King Solomon. Although known best for his legendary wisdom, Solomon was also the greatest, richest, and most powerful king of his day. Having succeeded his father David, who had built the kingdom of Israel into a great power, Solomon expanded his kingdom's greatness and glory even more. At no time in its history was Israel bigger, richer, or more powerful than under Solomon's reign.

Solomon's reputation was so great that even the queen of Sheba, way down in her African domain, heard of it. She immediately decided to visit Solomon and see for herself.

> *When the queen of Sheba heard about the fame of Solomon and his relation to the name of the Lord, she came to test him with hard questions. Arriving at Jerusalem with a very great caravan—with camels carrying spices, large quantities of gold, and precious stones—she came to Solomon and talked with him about all that she had on her mind. Solomon answered all her questions; nothing was too hard for the king to explain to her. When the queen of Sheba saw all the wisdom of Solomon and the palace he had built, the food on his table, the seating of his officials, the attending servants in their robes, his cup-bearers, and the burnt offerings he made at the temple of the Lord, she was overwhelmed. She said to the king, "The report I heard in my own country about your achievements and your wisdom is true. But I did not believe these things until I came and saw them with my own eyes. Indeed, not even half was told me; in wisdom and wealth you have far exceeded the report I heard"* (I Kings 10:1-7).

The queen of Sheba was a rich and powerful monarch in her own right, but everything she had and had always known paled in comparison to the splendor of Solomon's court. There was no sign of poverty anywhere in the land, because the citizens of Solomon's kingdom reflected in their lives and circumstances the splendor and wealth of Solomon himself. The rest of First Kings chapter 10 goes into a detailed description of the extent and glory of Solomon's kingdom. He was *"greater in riches and wisdom than all the other kings of the earth"* (I Kings 10:23), so rich, in fact, that he *"made silver as common in Jerusalem as stones"* (I Kings 10:27a). Prosperity was everywhere. Can you imagine the housekeeper wearing silk or the household servants eating off of gold plates? This is the way kingdoms manifest. A wise and conscientious king makes sure that his citizens prosper because he knows that his reputation and the glory of his rule rest on the quality of their lives.

In the 21st chapter of the Book of Revelation, John describes the New Jerusalem, the city of the King, as having a wall of jasper with the wall's foundations adorned with 12 kinds of precious stones (see verses 18-20). The city itself and its great street were made of pure gold. My point is this: The idea of earthly kings extravagantly displaying their wealth and splendor originated with God. Likewise, the splendor and glory of God's Kingdom will be reflected in the lives and circumstances of His citizens.

We have to change our mindset and learn to think like royalty. We must learn to see things from our King's perspective. Once my wife and I visited Buckingham Palace in London. Beginning with the lush gardens, everything about the place spoke of riches, dignity, honor, glory, and splendor. We walked into an entry foyer larger and more extravagant than the lobbies of the finest hotels in the world. The walls and ceiling were painted with gold leaf. You and I use latex paint on our walls, but the palace was painted in gold. Why would someone put gold all over the walls? To display to all visitors the splendor and glory of those who live there, even if they are never seen.

Buckingham Palace had a crystal chandelier larger than my living room. In a kingdom it is never necessary to talk or preach about prosperity because prosperity is all around. Prince William grew up looking at that chandelier. That is why his mentality is different from ours. You and I grew up under the illumination of Sylvania Blue Dot light bulbs. How could we talk with him about wealth? When you are born into wealth, you don't talk about wealth. God's ultimate goal is to bring that kind of life to Earth.

It is for this reason that Jesus taught us to pray to the Father, *"Your kingdom come, Your will be done on earth as it is in heaven"* (Matt. 6:10). Every other prayer we pray should be tempered by this one request: that God's heavenly Kingdom come on Earth. When we pray for the Kingdom, our prayer encompasses all we could ever need or desire, because with the Kingdom comes access to all the resources of Heaven. This is why Jesus also told us not to worry about what we would eat, drink, or wear, or about any other thing, but to seek first the King-dom and righteousness of God, for with the Kingdom comes everything else (see Matt. 6:33). Our future is tied up in the culture of the King. Therefore our prayer should be, "Lord, let Your Kingdom be manifested in us. Make us into a community that represents Your country and Your culture. May our common unity be a reflection of Your glory to a watching world."

COMMON UNITY

As I said earlier, the word *community* is a compound of the words "com-mon" and "unity." So even the derivation of the word *community* gives us a clue to its meaning: a group of people united by common bonds. More specifically, a community is a group of people distinguished and unified by a common set of values, standards, beliefs, norms, language, customs, traditions, ideals, and commitment to a common purpose.

Chinatown is a community. Its inhabitants are united by the common bond of their Chinese heritage and culture, which they keep vibrantly alive. China-town could never exist with only one or two, or even a handful of Chinese. Maintaining a distinct cultural identity requires a large number of people of similar background working together in a common purpose. In Los Angeles, the population of Chinatown is around 500,000 people. They speak their own language, worship in their own temples, operate their own businesses, and main-tain their own distinctive cuisine. Theirs is an unmistakably unique community, a "garden" of China within the United States.

Kingdom communities, wherever they are in the world, should be just as unique and distinctive. Our values, standards, beliefs, norms, language, customs, traditions, and ideals should set us apart from the rest of the world. People who walk into our community should feel like they have stepped into Heaven.

This is one reason why I have such a big problem with "religious" Christianity. Religion can never take the place of the Kingdom. Although it may try to mimic Kingdom characteristics on the outside, it is only a shallow and empty facade. Whenever I walk into Chinatown, I feel like I am in China. When I walk into Haitian Town, I feel like I am in Haiti. Miami's Cuban district makes me think I have somehow stepped into Havana. Whenever I walk into religious Christianity, however, I feel like I am in hell: cursing, gossiping, backbiting, lying, cheating, stealing, adultery, divorce, homosexuality, legalism, prejudice, self-righteousness, infighting, bickering—a real mess.

Religious Christianity looks nothing like Heaven. There is no unity, no common vision, no community. On the contrary, divisions abound, and each group is proud of its own exclusiveness. They divide and fight over doctrinal differences, theological differences, modes of baptism, spiritual gifts, theories of the end times, worship styles, worship music, biblical interpretation, and even about whether Saturday or Sunday is the "proper" worship day. Amidst such squabbling, how can there be community? I have a dream that before I die, there will be a group of people on Earth who finally get the message that the Kingdom of Heaven is bigger than our differences and broader than our denominations.

A Kingdom community is a group of Kingdom citizens who are unified by a common set of values—the King's values. They share the King's standards and beliefs and live according to the King's norms. They speak the language of the King, which is the language of love. In addition, they follow the customs and traditions of the King. They forgive one another. They love their enemies. They do good to those who mistreat them. They never engage in slander or gossip. They are honest in all their dealings and always keep their word. They respect the dignity of all people and hold all people in high regard as precious creatures made in God's image. They love God with all their heart and they love and honor His Word.

They also are committed to the King's ideals, meaning that they share a common ideology, or philosophy, with the King. In other words, they think like the King and share the same mindset. This is a learning process of growth and maturity, because none of us naturally think the way God does:

> *"For My thoughts are not your thoughts, neither are your ways My ways,"* declares the Lord. *"As the heavens are higher than the earth, so are My ways higher than your ways and My thoughts than your thoughts"*(Isaiah 55:8-9).

In a Kingdom community, all the citizens are learning to submit their minds and thoughts to the King so that they can learn to see as He sees, think as He thinks, and do as He does.

Finally, a Kingdom community is committed to a common purpose and vision—those of the King. A common vision brings a community into unity and helps guarantee its survival, because without vision a community will perish (see Prov. 29:18 KJV). And what is the King's vision? It is very simple: His Kingdom come and His will be done on Earth as it is in Heaven. God's vision—His big idea—is Heaven coming to Earth. He sees it. Can you see it?

Can you see Heaven's culture coming to Earth? Can you imagine a community where every husband loves his wife the way Christ loves His Church, and treats her like the queen she is? Can you imagine a community where every wife honors, respects, and builds up her husband? Can you imagine a community where husbands and wives are absolutely faithful to each other and where adultery or sweethearting is inconceivable? Can you imagine a community where all the children honor and obey their parents and show respect to all legitimate authority? Can you imagine a community where people's word is their bond and where honesty is the common currency? Can you imagine a community where there is no cursing or gambling, no greed or thievery, no envy or jealousy, no backbiting or backstabbing, no petty bickering or quarreling, and no lust or sexual immorality? Can you imagine a community where there is no poverty or want, but abundant peace and contentment? Can you imagine it? God can, and this is the type of community He wants to fill the Earth with.

TAKE A LESSON FROM THE JEWS

If there is any group of people on Earth who understand the power of community, it is the Jews. Through 4,000 years of war and conquest, peace and prosperity, persecution and prejudice, and triumph and tragedy, the Jews have maintained a distinct cultural identity as a people. This is due in large part to the fact that they identify themselves not only as individuals but also as interdependent members of a larger community.

The first five books of the Bible are political books, not religious treatises. They explain how God's purpose for delivering the Israelites from slavery in Egypt was to transform them into a nation through whom He would bless the world, just as He had promised Abraham (see Gen. 12:1-3). According to God's plan they would be a distinct people, separate from the other nations of the world in their worship, their laws, their morality, their diet, their code of conduct, and their everyday lifestyle. The distinguishing characteristic that would set them apart from other peoples would be God's active and continuing presence among them. Without His presence, they would be no different from any other nation. It was his awareness of this distinction that prompted Moses to pray:

> *If Your Presence does not go with us, do not send us up from here. How will anyone know that You are pleased with me and with Your people unless You go with us? What else will distinguish me and Your people from all the other people on the face of the earth?* (Exodus 33:15b-16)

In response the Lord assured Moses that His presence would go with them. We can ask the same question about Kingdom communities. What will distinguish us from other peoples and cultural groups on Earth if it is not the active and powerful presence of God in our everyday lives and activities?

Along with the preserving power of God, Jews have survived throughout the centuries as a distinct people because of their strong sense of community. If a Jew is financially broke, the community will come together and give him money to start a business so he won't be broke any longer. Jewish businessmen go to

Jewish attorneys for their legal work. Jewish mothers take their babies to Jewish pediatricians. Jewish bakers get their flour from Jewish mills. There is nothing prejudicial in this. They simply know that they are part of a community and live accordingly. They know that if they band together, everybody prospers.

Why don't believers and followers of Christ do the same? We have no sense of community. We are splintered by race and religion and by economics and ethnic background. Sometimes we are divided by pure jealousy. We are so caught up in the "every man for himself" mentality of the world that we won't take our business to a fellow believer because our attitude is, "I'm not going to help make him rich." That is foolishness.

Brothers and sisters, as Kingdom citizens, we are a community, and we are dependent on one another. We bear mutual responsibility for each other's welfare, success, and prosperity. The New Testament makes it abundantly clear that the early Christians saw themselves as a community as much as they saw themselves as individual believers. They shared common property so that no one went without. They distributed food to the needy and took care of widows and orphans. When the mostly Jewish church in Jerusalem was impoverished by persecution, Gentile churches throughout Asia Minor gave sacrificially, sometimes out of their own poverty, to bring relief to their Jewish brothers and sisters in Jerusalem.

We have somehow forgotten a truth that the early believers took to heart: united we stand, but divided we fall. The first-century church faced a world hostile to their message—in many ways as hostile as today's world is toward "Christianity"—yet they turned their world upside down in spite of it. How? In the power of the Spirit of God, certainly. But also because they banded together as a community, regardless of how far apart they were geographically. They took care of each other out of love and because they knew that no one else in this world would do it.

There is no logical reason why we could not do the same today. How hard would it be for a community of believers to commit together to support one another in every arena of life? Born-again business people would take their legal work to born-again attorneys. Believers with medical needs would consult born-again physicians. Believers would support believers, patronizing each others' businesses, pharmacies, grocery stores, bakeries, barber shops, beauty shops, gas stations, restaurants, building contractors, banks, and consulting, architectural, investment counseling, health care, dental, and optometry services, and the like. Some communities already publish directories of local and regional businesses and services owned by believers for this very purpose, but the practice needs to become much more widespread.

This does not mean that as Kingdom citizens we should separate ourselves from unbelievers. After all, how will they learn about the Kingdom unless we are around to tell them? But as we go among them day by day, we must never forget that we are not independent, but part of an interdependent community. The New Testament church had a strong sense of community, but they also reached out to the unbelieving world around them. There is no reason why we cannot do the same.

A HIGHER STANDARD

Scripture leaves no doubt that God's desire is to build a community of His people on Earth. Isaac, before sending his son Jacob to live with his mother's people, blessed him with these words: *"May God Almighty bless you and make you fruitful and increase your numbers until you become a community of peoples"* (Gen. 28:3).

Years later, in fulfillment of Isaac's blessing, God Himself promised Jacob:

> *I am God Almighty; be fruitful and increase in number. A nation and a community of nations will come from you, and kings will come from your body. The land I gave to Abraham and Isaac I also give to you, and I will give this land to your descendants after you* (Genesis 35:11-12).

Again, many years later, Jacob told his son Joseph about God's promise:

> *Jacob said to Joseph, "God Almighty appeared to me at Luz in the land of Canaan, and there He blessed me and said to me, 'I am going to make you*

fruitful and increase your numbers. I will make you a community of peoples, and I will give this land as an everlasting possession to your descendants after you'"(Genesis 48:3-4).

This promise of God to Jacob was fulfilled with the creation of the nation of Israel. As Kingdom citizens and members of the *ekklesia* of Jesus Christ, we are the spiritual descendants of Abraham, Isaac, Jacob, and the Israelite nation, so the promise is for us as well. This is doubly true because God's purpose never changes, and He has always purposed to build a community of His people on Earth.

But if we are going to become a Kingdom community, we must commit ourselves to a higher standard than that of the rest of the world. If we are going to represent God, our King, on Earth, we must hold to standards that faithfully represent Him and reflect His character. We need to heed Paul's wise counsel: *"Therefore, as we have opportunity, let us do good to all people, especially to those who belong to the family of believers"* (Gal. 6:10). God wants to bless us, but to be blessed we must obey His Word and live according to His standards. God wants to bless us, but His purpose in blessing us is to make us a community that will reach out and draw others in.

This is why in our Kingdom community there must be no hint of evil, dishonesty, corruption, selfishness, greed, or envy. The world is full of these things, and people are looking for something different. Besides, when we live this way, we reflect the character of our Lord, which is what we are after. Simon Peter, one of Christ's apostles, provides a vivid picture of what the life and character of a Kingdom community and its citizens should look like:

> *His divine power has given us everything we need for life and godliness through our knowledge of Him who called us by His own glory and goodness. Through these He has given us His very great and precious promises, so that through them you may participate in the divine nature and escape the corruption in the world caused by evil desires. For this very reason, make every effort to add to your faith goodness; and to goodness, knowledge; and to knowledge, self-control;*

and to self-control, perseverance; and to perseverance, godliness; and to godliness, brotherly kindness; and to brotherly kindness, love. For if you possess these qualities in increasing measure, they will keep you from being ineffective and unproductive in your knowledge of our Lord Jesus Christ. But if anyone does not have them, he is nearsighted and blind, and has forgotten that he has been cleansed from his past sins. Therefore, my brothers, be all the more eager to make your calling and election sure. For if you do these things, you will never fall, and you will receive a rich welcome into the eternal kingdom of our Lord and Savior Jesus Christ (2 Peter 1:3-11).

As a Kingdom community, we are held to a higher standard than that of the world. Religious communities often adapt and conform to the world's standards, which is one reason they are such a mess. Kingdom communities, on the other hand, do not accommodate; they elevate. They hold out the standards of the King without compromise and elevate to that level all who enter. That's the only way it can be.

COMMUNITY RESPONSIBILITY

One characteristic that distinguishes a Kingdom community from any other is that in a Kingdom community sins may be personal, but never private. The actions of one affect the whole. For the sake of the health and welfare of the community, God laid out a radical solution:

> *But if a person who is unclean does not purify himself, he must be cut off from the community, because he has defiled the sanctuary of the Lord. The water of cleansing has not been sprinkled on him, and he is unclean* (Numbers 19:20).

Sanctuary means the place where God lives. In a Kingdom community, God lives in His people, and the whole community is the palace of the Governor. Anyone who becomes a cancer to the body of the community must be cut off for the good of the community.

This may be a hard statement for many of us to accept, because we are so accustomed to hearing how loving God is, and how forgiving, kind and merciful, and tender He is. All these things are true, but they are beside the point. God certainly loves everyone, even the offenders, but His love and commitment to His community are so great that He will take radical steps to prevent it from being infected and destroyed from within. This is why Achan was stoned to death for violating God's ban on taking spoils from Jericho (see Josh. 7:25-26). This is why Paul commanded the Corinthian church to expel the incestuous member from its midst (see I Cor. 5:1-13). This is why Ananias and Sapphira died for lying to the Holy Spirit (see Acts 5:1-11). The Lord is jealous for His community and will do whatever He must to protect it and preserve its integrity.

Even worldly communities separate offenders by putting them in jail. How much more should we expect God to protect the purity of His community? The difference is that worldly communities lock offenders away to keep them from continually breaking the law, but those communities have no sense of sharing responsibility for the offenders' actions. In a Kingdom community, everyone bears responsibility for the actions of everyone else.

By the same token, in a Kingdom community, everyone bears one another's burdens. Paul said:

> *Brothers, if someone is caught in a sin, you who are spiritual should restore him gently. But watch yourself, or you also may be tempted. Carry each other's burdens, and in this way you will fulfill the law of Christ* (Galatians 6:1-2).

While Paul tells us to restore an offender "gently," it may be necessary first to separate that person from the community for a time until he or she responds to the Holy Spirit's prompting and repents.

In a Kingdom community, Kingdom citizens have no independent life. This is a particularly hard concept to grasp for those who have grown up under democratic and capitalistic systems where personal independence is regarded as one of the highest values of all. As Kingdom citizens, we are all in this together.

We need each other. We are all members of one body, and every member is vital for the proper functioning of that body. That is why an "illness" that infects one of us infects all of us. And that is why we cannot afford to ignore or write off any member of the community.

If any of us are going to represent Heaven, all of us must represent Heaven. If your brother in the Lord is weak, it is your responsibility to help strengthen him. If your sister in the Lord is going through a struggle, call her and say, "Honey, stay strong. I am with you, and so is the Lord. Don't compromise. We're together in this." Then pray with her. We must all help each other be strong in order to protect everybody and preserve the integrity of the community.

And God's promise is that if His Kingdom citizens live right, He will give them "diplomatic immunity": immunity from sickness, disease, poverty. The entire community will prosper, and everyone outside will want to know why. "How come everybody got fired except you?" "Well, I have diplomatic immunity." "How come everybody else's business is shutting down, but yours is prospering?" "I have diplomatic immunity." "Why did my crop fail but yours didn't?" "I have diplomatic immunity." "How can you be doing so well when the economy is in such bad shape?" "I have diplomatic immunity." "How can you be so calm, so at peace, and so joyful when the world is going to hell in a hand basket?" "I have diplomatic immunity."

The world can't help but be attracted to a Kingdom community that lives like the Kingdom whose name it bears, because there is nothing else in the world like it. That is why we must be so careful to live with integrity and without compromise and to strike the proper balance between being in the world as a community of believers, but not of the world. We cannot reach the world with the message of the Kingdom if we shut ourselves off from the world. We must relate to the world through the Kingdom principle of *engagement*.

Chapter Nine

ENGAGING THE
POPULAR CULTURE

THE Kingdom principle of engagement is simply defined as influencing the popular culture through the community of faith. As I have mentioned elsewhere in this book, all humans are searching for meaning in their lives. We all want to know that there is a reason and a purpose for our existence; that we were not born by accident. Throughout the ages, human philosophers have sought to understand life and therefore find meaning in it. Religion has tried to do the same thing. Regardless of their culture, people all over the world look at their surroundings and circumstances and ask, "Is this all?" They examine their day-to-day experiences and think, "Certainly there is more to life than this."

By and large, however, man's search for meaning has come up empty because he has failed or refused to look for meaning and purpose in the one place in the universe he can find them: the Kingdom of Heaven. As Kingdom citizens and members of the Kingdom community, we not only possess the answer to humanity's search for meaning, but we also bear the responsibility of sharing it with others. The only way for the Kingdom community to bring its influence to bear in the world is by engaging the popular culture on equal terms on a consistent, day-by-day basis. In order to do this, we must each be committed to representing the nature and character of our King and to living His culture daily before the world with boldness and without apology or compromise.

Man's search for meaning is all about his quest for a lost inheritance. Philosophy can't find it. Science can't find it. Religion can't find it. Only those who are citizens of the Kingdom of Heaven have found it, because the King Himself has restored it. In fact, the Kingdom itself is the inheritance, and with the Kingdom comes everything else. Possession of the inheritance is what distinguishes the Kingdom community and its citizens from all other communities and peoples on Earth. The King desires for every person in the world to become a citizen of His community and to receive his or her inheritance. The day is coming when the King Himself will separate forever those who are His citizens from those who are not. In the meantime, He has charged His citizens with the commission to engage the world and proclaim His Kingdom by both word and lifestyle so that as many as possible of the people of the world will transfer their citizenship from the pretender's kingdom to His.

Although we will not experience the complete fullness of our inheritance until we enter the life to come, as Kingdom citizens, our inheritance is a present reality. In fact, Kingdom community life is the daily living out of our inheritance in real and practical ways. Jesus described it this way:

> *When the Son of man comes in His glory, and all the angels with Him, He will sit on His throne in heavenly glory. All the nations will be gathered before Him, and He will separate the people one from another as a shepherd separates the sheep from the goats. He will put the sheep on His right and the goats on His left. Then the king will say to those on His right, "Come, you who are blessed by My Father; take your inheritance, the kingdom prepared for you since the creation of the world. For I was hungry and you gave Me something to eat, I was thirsty and you gave Me something to drink, I was a stranger and you invited Me in, I needed clothes and you clothed Me, I was sick and you looked after Me, I was in prison and you came to visit Me."*

Then the righteous will answer Him, "Lord, when did we see You hungry and feed You, or thirsty and give You something to drink? When did we see You a stranger and invite You in, or needing clothes and clothe You? When did we see You sick or in prison and go to visit You?"

The King will reply, "I tell you the truth, whatever you did for one of the least of these brothers of Mine, you did for Me" (Matthew 25:31-40).

We have not inherited a religion. Cultures and societies may transfer religions from one generation to the next, but that is not our inheritance. Our inheritance is the Kingdom—not just any kingdom, but *the* Kingdom. What Adam lost, Christ has restored to us. Rulership is in our genes, authority, in our very makeup. We were designed to rule the Earth. The Kingdom is the rightful inheritance of all humankind. Many people, however, do not know this, which is why we of the Kingdom community must engage those who live in the world's culture. They need to be informed of their inheritance.

As Kingdom citizens, our goal should be to stay in touch with Heaven every moment of every day. It is for this reason that God sent His Holy Spirit not to visit us but to live inside of us, so He could guide us into the knowledge of all truth and teach us how to live and act and talk like the King.

This is the way—and the only way—for us to exert a continuing influence and make a permanent impact for the Kingdom in the popular culture. In order to transform the popular culture, we must engage the popular culture, and we can engage it successfully only in the Spirit, likeness, and power of our King.

HEAVEN IS NOT OUR PRIORITY

When talking about the Kingdom principle of engagement, it is important that we first understand what our assignment is not. Because there is so much confusion on this issue, we need to be absolutely clear about what we are not supposed to do.

1. God did not assign us to go to Heaven. Despite what many churches and denominations teach, going to Heaven is not our priority. As I have said before and throughout this book, most religions, including religious Christianity, focus on teaching their people how to get ready to escape Earth and go to Heaven, however they conceive Heaven to be. That is not our assignment as Kingdom citizens. Remember, God did not create the world to be empty, but to be inhabited (see Isa. 45:18). *"The highest heavens belong to the Lord, but the earth He has given to man"* (Ps. 115:16). In other words, Heaven should not be our passion or ultimate goal, but rather, the bringing of Heaven to Earth.

2. God did not assign us to prepare others to "go to Heaven." He assigned us to tell others about the Kingdom of Heaven that has come to Earth, and then, once their hunger for the Kingdom has been stirred up, to tell them how they can enter the Kingdom through faith in Christ. We talk so much about "witnessing" to people to try to get them into Heaven. That is the wrong emphasis. When we study the ministry of Jesus Christ, we discover that He was not after trying to get people into Heaven. He was bringing the Kingdom of Heaven to Earth and was after getting people into the Kingdom. We talk about the importance of being "born again," and then stop, as if that is all there is to it. Jesus Himself linked the new birth with the Kingdom when He said, *"I tell you the truth, no one can see the kingdom of God unless he is born again"* (John 3:3). Our assignment is not to help people to prepare for Heaven, but to help them enter the Kingdom of Heaven.

3. God did not assign us to establish a religion. As I have stressed over and over, creating a religion was never part of God's plan, and Jesus never established one either. Religion is man's creation, not God's. In the beginning God established His Kingdom on Earth and gave man dominion over it. Man lost his earthly Kingdom, and Christ came to bring it back. When Jesus came to Earth He did not bring a religion; He re-established the rule and government of His Father. Then He established His *ekklesia*, His Church, to sustain and expand that government throughout the world. The Kingdom of Heaven is not about religion, but relationship: a King relating to His children. And although it has government and law, the Kingdom of Heaven is not about legalism, but lifestyle.

4. *God did not assign us to promote a religion or a denomination.* We all know that there are people who are willing to fight and even die for their religion. Throughout human history, more wars have been fought over religion than any other single cause. People get upset when you touch their religion. Think of the Muslims in Europe and other parts of the world who rioted after a Danish newspaper published unflattering cartoons of Muhammad. Think of the violence and hostility that occurs between the Sunni and Shiite sects of Islam. Think about the Christians who get upset every time some unbeliever makes a disparaging comment in the news about God, Christ, the Church, or a particular denomination. Think about all the infighting that goes on between denominations over baptism, church polity and government, which day is the "true" Lord's Day, theology, doctrine, and biblical interpretation. Religions are always fighting because they are not under the Kingdom. Our assignment is not to promote a religion or a denomination, but to proclaim the Kingdom. There is only one Kingdom, and one King, and within His government, there is no debate, no division, and no disunity.

THE WORLD IS NOT OUR ENEMY

Just as Heaven is not our priority, neither is the world our enemy. Although as Kingdom citizens we are not *of* the world, we are *in* the world, and it is God's will that we engage the world's culture with the principles, claims, and authority of the Kingdom of Heaven.

5. *God did not assign us to separate or isolate ourselves from the world.* This is a big hang-up for many believers. In our desire to be holy, we become "holier than thou" by trying to have nothing to do with unbelievers. "We don't mix with ungodly people." "I will not go into a room where people are smoking." "I can't be seen with you because your skirt is too short." "I don't hang around with people who drink and cuss all the time." Many believers would rather spend

all their time around other believers, even to the point of desiring to work at a Christian job for a Christian boss at a Christian company. We cannot engage the popular culture by escaping from it, nor can we influence it by isolating ourselves from it. Jesus certainly didn't. One of the biggest criticisms the religious leaders leveled against Jesus was the fact that He spent so much time with "sinners," the dirty, disreputable, and cast-off dregs of society. When challenged on this, He responded,

> *"It is not the healthy who need a doctor, but the sick. But go and learn what this means: 'I desire mercy, not sacrifice.' For I have not come to call the righteous, but sinners"* (Matthew 9:12-13).

That is our assignment too.

6. *God did not assign us to attack or condemn the world.* From the way some believers talk, you would think that our number one job is to pronounce judgment on the world. No, our job is not judgment but influence. Our job is to do what Jesus did, and even He did not come to judge the world. A day is coming when Christ will return as Judge, but He came the first time not to judge the world but to save it:

> *For God so loved the world that He gave His one and only Son, that whoever believes in Him shall not perish but have eternal life. For God did not send His Son into the world to condemn the world, but to save the world through Him* (John 3:16-17).

We accomplish nothing by attacking and condemning people for their sins. Deep in their hearts, unbelievers know they are sinners. They know their lives are messed up and out of alignment with God. They don't need us in our self-righteousness laying it out for them, especially if we come off sounding like we think we are beyond those kinds of things. They know better. We can't draw people to the Kingdom by offending them with our manner. (Becoming offended by our message, however, is another matter entirely.) In order to influence them, we must show patience and sensitivity.

7. *God did not assign us to compete with the world.* Sometimes we act as though we believe that our job is to keep up with the world, that every pronouncement or production of the world requires a "Christian" response. We assume that the Kingdom of Heaven must be defended and that no challenge should go unmet. This is faulty thinking. Christ never tried to keep up with the Roman Empire. Why not? Because He knew there was no competition. This is why He told Pilate,

> *My kingdom is not of this world. If it were, My servants would fight to prevent My arrest by the Jews. But now My kingdom is from another place* (John 18:36).

There is no need for us to "defend" the Kingdom; that is not our job. The King is perfectly capable of defending His own Kingdom. Our assignment is not to compete with the world, because there is no competition. We are from a different country than those who are of the world. Our job is not to compete, but to manifest the Kingdom in our lives and let the Kingdom speak for itself.

8. *God did not assign us to avoid the world.* Because of the escapist mentality that is taught by many churches and denominations, many believers have virtually written off any chance or effort of trying to change the world. They have essentially surrendered to the opposition in the areas of politics, education, the media, and every other institution of cultural formation and influence, and now consign themselves to "spiritual" pursuits while waiting for Christ to come and rescue them out of the world. Throughout this book, we have seen the fallacy of this line of thinking. As Kingdom citizens, we are in the world for a reason, not to avoid the world, but to do our part to influence and change the world through our personal involvement. Run for the school board so you can help monitor what kinds of textbooks come into the classrooms in your community. Get involved in politics. Run for office, or at the very least, vote regularly. Read up on current issues, and stay abreast of the news. Choose a "secular" career that will get you into the mainstream of society where your influence can be the greatest. Get involved in education. Get involved in business. Get involved

in entertainment. Get involved in every area of law and medicine. We cannot engage the popular culture by avoiding it; we must fill it with Kingdom people.

ENGAGING THE WORLD IS OUR PRIORITY

God did not place us on Earth as His people just so we could start getting ready to leave. He placed us here to plant and reproduce gardens of His Kingdom throughout the world, thereby reclaiming and transforming territory laid waste by the pretender's rapacious rule. Having examined what we were *not* assigned to do, it is time to look more specifically at the assignments our King *has* given us. Here is what we are *supposed* to be doing.

I. *God assigned us to reintroduce the Kingdom to the world.* Jesus set the stage. He laid the groundwork when He first appeared in His public ministry proclaiming a simple, straightforward message: *"Repent, for the kingdom of heaven is near"* (Matt. 4:17). He called followers to Himself and established His Church, His *ekklesia*, His "called-out ones," to continue the work He began, to preach the same message, and to carry out the same assignment. That is why He told His disciples,

> I tell you the truth, anyone who has faith in Me will do what I have been doing. He will do even greater things than these, because I am going to the Father (John 14:12).

People all over the world are searching for the Kingdom even though they don't know it. We who are of the Kingdom bear the responsibility of helping them find it. Our assignment is linked to the timing of Christ's return and the end of the age: *"And this gospel of the kingdom will be preached in the whole world as a testimony to all nations, and then the end will come"* (Matt. 24:14).

2. *God assigned us to repossess the earth with the Kingdom.* Psalm 24:1 says, *"The earth is the Lord's, and everything in it, the world, and all who live in it."* Psalm 115:16 adds, *"The highest heavens belong to the Lord, but the earth He has given to man."* These verses are still true because God never changes, and His gifts and calling are irrevocable (see Rom. 11:29). Yet for

thousands of years the Earth effectively has been under the rule and sway of satan the pretender. Christ's death and resurrection broke satan's power and put him on notice of eviction. He restored the Kingdom of Heaven on earth to its rightful human overlords. Now, like the ancient Israelites after they crossed the Jordan River to take possession of the land of Canaan, as God had promised, it is time for us as Kingdom citizens to fully repossess the territory that is rightfully ours. We do this not by separation but by infiltration.

3. *God assigned us to engage the world system.* Engagement means involvement. Battles in wartime are often called engagements. To engage something means to meet it head on, to confront it and challenge it without backing down and without surrender. Popular society and culture will never be changed by those who refuse to engage them. It has been said that all that is necessary for evil to triumph is for good people to do nothing. Evil has held sway in the world for far too long. People need to know that life has meaning and purpose. They need to know that there is an alternative to the seemingly unending cycle of hatred, violence, cruelty, poverty, and misery. They need to be given reason for hope. Our assignment is to infuse the popular culture with the values, morals, and standards of the Kingdom of God. One way to do this is by working diligently for the passage of laws that uphold standards, and for the election of public officials who will do the same. The reason is simple: whoever controls the laws controls the culture. That is why the first thing God did after delivering the Israelites from Egyptian slavery was to give them a code of law. In order to make them into a nation, He needed to reshape their slave culture and mindset into the culture and mindset of people of God. Our purpose in engaging the world system is the same.

4. *God assigned us to influence the world, not to keep up with it.* It is impossible to change a culture by accommodating it. Yet that is exactly what countless churches and believers have tried to do, to their own detriment. The only thing we accomplish by accommodating culture is to become like the very culture we are trying to change. Rather than transforming culture, when we accommodate, we allow the popular culture to transform us into its own image. The secret to effective influence is to remain distinct. The standards and principles of the Kingdom of Heaven are diametrically opposed to those of the world system. When people in that system see Kingdom communities where Kingdom citizens are living according to Kingdom principles, the difference will be so stark as to be unmistakable. And when they see that Kingdom communities actually work, and bring about an environment and lifestyle of peace, joy, contentment, and prosperity unlike anything found in the world, they will find it irresistible.

CHANGING THE WORLD IS OUR GOAL

Our assignment is nothing less than to change the world; and to do that, we have to become involved with the world.

5. *God assigned us to affect the world, not reject the world.* When humankind chose to disobey God and reject His rule, God would have been perfectly within His rights as Creator to reject us, destroy us, and start all over. But He did not do that. He chose to pursue us in spite of our sin and woo and win us back to Him; and He did this by direct involvement. Through His Son Jesus Christ, the King injected Himself directly into the world system, to change it not by war and conquest, but by influence, by the gradual infiltration and manifestation of His power and presence in the lives of individuals. Jesus went directly and deliberately to the castoffs of society,

the people whom even the religious leaders—*especially* the religious leaders—wanted nothing to do with. He related to each one on a personal basis. In the same way, we are to spread Kingdom influence throughout the world—one person at a time.

6. *God assigned us to revolutionize the world.* As Kingdom citizens we are revolutionaries, because our Lord was a revolutionary. Christ never led an armed revolt against the Romans, but His life and teachings were revolutionary in their effect. Unlike other revolutionaries, however, who always seek to establish new ideas, Jesus' goal was to re-establish an *old* idea, God's original big idea of Heaven on Earth. His strategy was to employ words rather than warfare and influence instead of invasion. This is why He commonly made statements like: "You have heard that it was said...but I tell you...." He was applying a corrective. He was replacing bad ideas with good ideas and wrong thinking with right thinking. True revolutions begin by changing people's thinking; only then do they translate to action. We will change the world the same way: by word, example, and influence.

7. *God assigned us to occupy the Earth, not abandon it.* God created the Earth to be inhabited, and He created us in His own image to be its inhabitants. His original mandate to us, which has never changed, was that we be fruitful and multiply, and that we fill the Earth and subdue it; in short, that we exercise dominion over it. So far, our overall track record under the pretender's influence has not been good, as we have abused and misused the Earth, its resources, its creatures, and our fellow humans. The purpose of Kingdom communities, God's gardens on Earth, is to correct and reverse that history. Our assignment is to occupy the Earth and fill it anew with the vibrant culture of Heaven, which gives life and purpose and value to everything it touches.

8.   G OD ASSIGNED US TO PROMOTE THE GOVERNMENT OF HEAVEN ON EARTH. WE ARE NOT HERE TO PROMOTE EITHER A RELIGION OR OURSELVES ANY MORE THAN JESUS DID. OUR ASSIGNMENT IS TO PROMOTE THE GOVERNMENT OF HEAVEN ON EARTH. THIS MEANS THAT WE NEED TO KEEP ON PROCLAIMING IT, DECLARING IT, AND LIVING IT WHEREVER WE GO. WE NEED TO PROMOTE THE KINGDOM IN OUR JOBS, BUSINESSES, FAMILIES, THROUGH OUR INVESTMENTS, AND IN OUR RELATIONSHIPS, MARRIAGES, AND PARENTING. WE MUST BRING THE KINGDOM INTO EVERYTHING, EVERY ARENA AND FACET OF LIFE. THE WORLD SHAMELESSLY PROMOTES ITS CULTURE. AS KINGDOM CITIZENS WE NEED TO BE JUST AS BOLD IN PROMOTING OURS. MINGLING WITH THE WEEDS

In Chapter Two I briefly discussed Jesus' parable of the wheat and the weeds as an illustration of the fact that two distinct cultures exist in the world: Kingdom culture and the culture of the pretender. I want to return to that parable in connection with the Kingdom principle of engagement—that we are to engage the popular culture rather than separate ourselves from it.

> *Jesus told them another parable: The kingdom of heaven is like a man who sowed good seed in his field. But while everyone was sleeping, his enemy came and sowed weeds among the wheat, and went away. When the wheat sprouted and formed heads, then the weeds also appeared. The owner's servants came to him and said, "Sir, didn't you sow good seed in your field? Where then did the weeds come from?"*
>
> *"An enemy did this," he replied.*
>
> *The servants asked him, "Do you want us to go and pull them up?"*
>
> *"No," he answered, "because while you are pulling the weeds, you may root up the wheat with them. Let both grow together until the harvest. At that time I will tell the harvesters: First collect the weeds and tie them in bundles*

to be burned; then gather the wheat and bring it into my barn" (Matthew 13:24-30).

As Jesus explained to His disciples later, the man who sowed the good seed represents the Son of Man, Jesus Himself; the enemy who sowed the weeds is the devil; the good seed represents children of the Kingdom, and the weeds, children of the devil (see Matt. 13:37-39).

The point I want us to understand here is that the wheat and the weeds—the children of the Kingdom and the children of the devil—are allowed to *grow together* until the harvest, which is the end of time. In other words, Kingdom citizens *mingle* with citizens of the world throughout history, and this is by the King's design. He has chosen deliberately to leave His children in the world, in the midst of the "weeds," so that we can make a difference in the lives of those weeds.

In strictly human terms, we all know that a weed cannot change into a stalk of wheat, but in God's Kingdom nothing is impossible. By His power working in and through the lives and influence of His people, God can convert useless weeds into purposeful wheat. He can transform dark, confused, broken, and unproductive people into persons full of purpose, abundant life, and fulfilled destiny. But He cannot work through us for this purpose unless we are in the world and among the weeds. That is the principle behind the Kingdom concept of engagement.

"Let both grow together until the harvest" (Matt. 13:30). The Lord has called us to engage the world and its people. Do the folks you work with curse or smoke or drink or shack up with men or women they are not married to? God says, "I want you to stay right there and shine the light of Kingdom culture on them." Does your job or everyday business dealings bring you into contact with people who use drugs? God says, "Stay right there. Let your righteous life influence them to seek My Kingdom." Our calling is not to hide from the world but to engage it for the Kingdom of Heaven. Jesus put it this way:

You are the salt of the earth. But if the salt loses its saltiness, how can it be made salty again? It is no longer good for anything, except to be thrown out and trampled by men. You are the light of the world. A city set on a hill cannot be hidden. Neither do people light a lamp and put it under a bowl. Instead they put it on its stand, and it gives light to everyone in the house. In the same way, let your light shine before men, that they may see your good deeds and praise your Father in heaven (Matthew 5:13-16).

Religion separates and isolates. The Kingdom engages. Just as a farmer sows his seed, so the King sprinkles His Kingdom citizens everywhere with an abundant harvest in mind. He is saying, "I am throwing you out; wherever you land, influence that place for Me. Don't isolate yourself. Don't stay away from folks who are not in the Kingdom. Get involved. Engage. Make an impact where you are. Be bold in My strength to confront the earthly powers of this present age. The world will soon see who is more powerful." The Kingdom of Heaven is not afraid of evil, and we who are its citizens need not fear it either, because the one who is in us is greater than the one who is in the world (see 1 John 4:4).

ENGAGEMENT WORKS LIKE YEAST

As we have already seen, Jesus also likened the Kingdom of Heaven to yeast that works silently but surely to completely transform the dough. This is exactly the way the Kingdom principle of engagement works. In fact, yeast has several interesting characteristics that illustrate how Kingdom engagement operates.

First, yeast is inactive when it is sealed in the package. It cannot do its work until it is released into the dough. It is the same way with us. We cannot exert our Kingdom influence if we isolate ourselves from the world by staying within the four walls of our homes or church buildings. We have to inject ourselves into the "dough" of the world if we are to do any good.

Second, yeast by itself looks helpless and insignificant. Once released, however, its influence far exceeds its initial outward appearance. In the same way, the most effective way we can be yeast in our culture is not to be loud, flashy, and flamboyant, but quiet and unassuming, yet faithfully, consistently, and steadily living and promoting the Kingdom day by day. After all, as the hare in Aesop's fable, "The Tortoise and the Hare" learned to his chagrin, "Slow and steady wins the race."

Third, yeast is not intimidated by the size of the dough. That tiny yeast will look at that big batch of dough and say, "I can eat you for lunch." It doesn't matter where God put you, how tough your situation looks, or how great your challenge appears to be. As a Kingdom citizen with the Governor living in you, you always have the edge.

Fourth, yeast is not influenced by the dough, but the dough is influenced by the yeast. Yeast never becomes dough, but dough becomes "yeast" dough— permeated with yeast's transforming effects. In the same way, through Kingdom engagement, the Kingdom never becomes like the world, but the world becomes like the Kingdom.

Fifth, yeast changes the condition of the dough. The longer yeast has to work, the greater the transformation of the dough. In the same way, the longer our influence is in a place, the more that place should become like the Kingdom of Heaven.

Sixth, yeast works quietly. It doesn't force anything; it just goes to work. Engagement doesn't mean browbeating people with the Bible or being intimidating or obnoxious in our promotion of the Kingdom. It means going to work quietly, steadily, and consistently. No noise, no fuss, no spectacle; just make Kingdom decisions and set a solid Kingdom example day in and day out. You are there to infect, not obstruct or distract. Eventually, someone will ask why you seem so different, and that will be your opening to talk about the Kingdom. But before you can talk the talk you have to walk the walk.

Seventh, all yeast has to do to work is show up. You don't have to tell yeast what to do. All you have to do is release it and let it work. By the same token, we should be "yeast" automatically wherever we are as we allow the Holy Spirit to "release" Himself and work in and through us.

Eighth, yeast is activated by heat. Putting it in hot water releases its power. In a similar way, pressure propels us toward maturity. It helps make us more effective. Are you under pressure right now? God is saying, "Don't run. Stay put and affect everything. Show them your attitude, your values, your morals, your standards. Let them see the Kingdom." Don't get mad; get ahead. The Kingdom is like yeast; it becomes more powerful under pressure.

Ninth, and finally, once yeast gets in the dough it can never ever be retracted or ignored. God's Kingdom is here on Earth to stay, and it will grow until it fills the Earth and accomplishes everything God has intended from the very beginning. As Kingdom citizens, we can exert an influence that is far greater and that will last far longer than anything we could ever do alone. That is why God has put each of us where we are right now. He needs and wants us where He has placed us. We are His secret weapons to engage the popular culture and transform it into a garden of His glory. However, being effective as yeast means learning the trick of how to live in two worlds on one Earth.

Chapter Ten

LIVING IN TWO WORLDS
ON ONE EARTH

K INGDOM citizens are people with their feet in two different worlds. One
  foot is planted squarely in the Kingdom community, where daily life is
ordered by the righteous principles, standards, and culture of God Almighty,
while the other stands securely in the society and culture of the world. At heart,
the two worlds are incompatible because they operate according to principles and
philosophies that are diametrically opposed to each other. Yet we live in both
worlds simultaneously. This is the challenge of living in the Kingdom. In order
to do so successfully, we have to understand the principles of Kingdom extension
and influence and how they work in conjunction with the present culture we are in.
How do we live in two worlds on one Earth? More importantly, how do we claim
one world—the popular culture—and bring it under Kingdom government?

Attitude is the key, and attitude determines strategy.

To begin with, we must have the proper attitude with regard to the Kingdom of Heaven and the kingdom of this world. The first is eternal, while the
second is temporal. In other words, though the Kingdom of Heaven will last
forever, the kingdom of this world will someday pass away to be replaced by a
new kingdom on a new Earth. Psalm 45:6 says, *"Your throne, O God, will last forever*

and ever; a scepter of justice will be the scepter of Your kingdom." A king's scepter is the symbol of his power, authority, and favor. Whoever has the scepter acts in the king's authority, and the one to whom the king holds out his scepter receives the king's favor. So the scepter represents the character of the king and his rule. Justice, then, is the character of God and His Kingdom.

Psalm 103:19 says, *"The Lord has established His throne in heaven, and His kingdom rules over all."* "All" means everything there is. There is nothing and no one anywhere over whom God does not rule. If justice is the character of God's Kingdom, then the universe in its entirety is the scope of God's Kingdom.

Psalm 145:13a says, *"Your kingdom is an everlasting kingdom, and Your dominion endures through all generations."* From eternity past to eternity future, God's Kingdom endures. If justice is the character of God's Kingdom, and the universe is its scope, then eternity is its duration.

Recognizing the just, universal, and eternal nature of the Kingdom of Heaven should inspire us to adjust our attitude to acknowledge that the kingdom of this world can never equal or compete with God's eternal Kingdom. The knowledge that we are citizens of a just Kingdom that can never be overthrown and will never pass away should give us boldness as we engage the kingdom of this world and its culture.

Whenever we pray, "Your kingdom come, and Your will be done on earth as it is in heaven," we are praying for the celestial to transform the terrestrial. Celestial means heavenly, invisible, and spiritual. As children of God created in His image and likeness, we have firm connections to both worlds. On the one hand, we are celestial, spiritual beings who will live forever, while on the other hand, our beings are housed in terrestrial, physical bodies of clay that will die and decay, only to be replaced by new bodies that will not. No other creatures in the whole of God's universal Kingdom have this dual celestial-terrestrial nature. So we are ideally suited by nature and design to be God's instruments to transform the terrestrial realm into the likeness of the celestial.

No Coexistence

One of the first attitude adjustments we must make is to get rid of our "religious" thinking. As I have stressed over and over, Kingdom living has nothing to do with religion. For one thing, religious thinking believes in coexistence; it makes room for everybody: every sect, every denomination, every belief system, every philosophy; those with high values and those with no values at all; those who believe in many gods, one god, or no god. Coexistence says, "Let's all try to get along. After all, there are many roads to the truth, and each road is just as valid as the next." Coexistence makes room for Islam, Hinduism, Buddhism, Judaism, Christianity, Christian Science, Scientology, Unitarianism, Bahai, Hare Krishna, witchcraft, animism, atheism, and all the rest. Coexistence regards accommodation as the highest value.

There is no such thing as coexistence in the Kingdom of Heaven. The Kingdom did not come to Earth to coexist; it came to take over and transform. In the Kingdom there is only one vision, one will, one standard, one law, one belief system, one value system, one moral code, one code of ethics, one code of conduct, and one culture—the King's. The existence of any other constitutes rebellion. If the King's word is law and absolute, how can there be multitudes of little "kingdoms" within the Kingdom? There can't be. Since there is only one King and only one Kingdom, coexistence is impossible.

We have already seen how Jesus likened the Kingdom of Heaven to yeast. Let's imagine for a moment that we have a large mixing bowl containing lumps of dough made from different kinds of flour: white, wheat, oat, rice, nut, etc. And let's imagine further that each of these lumps represents a "kingdom" of the world, whether a nation, a religion, or whatever. Now suppose that we mix yeast in with all those different lumps of dough. What do you think will happen? Do you think the yeast will discriminate between the different kinds of flour? Each kind of flour is different, but the yeast doesn't care; it ignores those distinctions, proceeds with its fermentation process, and transforms the entire batch of dough.

God's Kingdom is not here to coexist with the kingdoms of this world, but to supplant and transform them. The multi-faith rally in Mexico City that I attended and that I described in the beginning of Chapter One is a case in point. That rally was organized around the philosophy of coexistence. All of the world's major religions (and many of the minor ones) were represented, and each one was afforded equal dignity, respect, and honor. All the speakers were received respectfully and politely. But when I stood up and talked about the Kingdom—not religion—everyone in the arena was clamoring for more. Why? The message of the Kingdom is like yeast in the dough of religion and worldly kingdoms. Yeast doesn't believe in coexistence. It permeates and agitates and will not stop until it has transformed its environment into something completely new. The Kingdom of Heaven cannot simply and tidily be given a place sharing the stage with all the religions, philosophies, and faith systems of the world. It will grow and expand and overwhelm and transform until it alone is left.

So all who are Kingdom citizens face the dilemma and challenge of how to live successfully and simultaneously in two worlds that are in inevitable conflict. In Chapter Two we talked about the clash of cultures between the Kingdom and the world. One critical key to our successful navigation within these two worlds is to get it thoroughly into our heads that the Kingdom of Heaven is not a kingdom of coexistence but of transformation, and that it is the Kingdom, not the world, that will ultimately prevail. This understanding can help us develop the habit of thinking with a Kingdom mindset and making Kingdom decisions in every area of life.

As Kingdom citizens, we must be prepared for clash and conflict. We cannot enter the Kingdom of God and continue to live like our unsaved friends. All of a sudden everything changes: our culture, our nature, our interests, our priorities, our tastes—everything. We are new creations in Christ; the old is gone and everything has become new (see 2 Cor. 5:17). Our assignment on Earth is not coexistence, compromise, or half measures. It is total transformation. It is love taking over a love-starved planet.

KINGDOM TRANSFORMATION IN ACTION

We're not talking about theoretical concepts here, but principles that actually work in practical, everyday ways. For example, there is a woman in our congregation who not long ago took over as manager of a dying restaurant, and within six months, by applying Kingdom principles, turned it completely around. One of the first decisions she made as manager was to set a standard for all the workers—a Kingdom standard. She retrained all the staff and helped reignite their passion for their work and for the restaurant's success. Prior to her arrival, each of the chefs cooked everything, according to what came along. She organized them according to their gifts and abilities so that each chef prepared the dishes he or she was especially good at.

The restaurant had televisions that previously had been used to watch anything. This Kingdom manager established a policy that limited the television viewing to two channels: TBN (Trinity Broadcasting Network) and CNN. No one, including the customers, was allowed to change the channels. She did this so that as manager she could control and create an appropriate atmosphere. If a customer asked to change the channel, she politely and respectfully declined, saying that she appreciated the customer's business, but that those were the rules.

Her lifestyle of uncompromising but non-belligerent obedience to Kingdom principles even in the workplace brought about a transformation in the lives of her employees. Their attitudes and morale changed drastically as they observed the consistency and excellence of her management style and operating principles. She and her employees regularly pray together, and she testifies that today there is continual worship in both the kitchen and the office. In addition, the restaurant is closed on Sundays so that all the workers can go to their own houses of worship.

When this dedicated Kingdom citizen and servant took over, the restaurant was dying. Within months, the restaurant had become so popular that customers were waiting in line even before the 11 A.M. opening time, and on most days, from 11:30 A.M. to 3 P.M., the line is out the door. Income for the business has tripled since she became manager, enabling her to give generous raises to the employees. The business even bought one employee a car and gave computers to two of the student employees. Turnaround of workers is low, and the restaurant is now looking to expand into a franchise and even go international.

That is quite a transformation, from a single struggling restaurant to a successful and growing operation—and all because one dedicated Kingdom citizen determined to apply Kingdom principles, without compromise or coexistence, in the place where God had placed her.

Whenever the Kingdom comes into a place, it impacts and overrides the culture of that place, not with violence or heavy-handed tactics, but with love and an unshakable confidence in the absolute legitimacy, superiority, and supremacy of Kingdom government. We are not supposed to dress like the popular culture, or live like the popular culture, or take a light view of sex and morality like the popular culture. We are supposed to set the standard, the higher standard of the Kingdom. We are supposed to override the popular culture. We are supposed to exercise self-control and moderation in all things and impact the people around us. We should not allow the environment to change us.

Instead, we should change our environment and bring it into conformity with God's Kingdom. The apostle Paul said, *"Do not conform any longer to the pattern of this world, but be transformed by the renewing of your mind"* (Rom. 12:2a). Once transformed in this manner, we then transform our environment wherever we go until it is a clear reflection of the Kingdom.

No coexistence. Transformation of the popular culture will come only from communities of Kingdom citizens who refuse to remain silent, who refuse to sit idly by, uninvolved and disengaged, while the agents of the *"powers of this dark world and...the spiritual forces of evil in the heavenly realms"* (Eph. 6:12) set their agenda and run the show. We must speak up. We must step out. We must get involved. We must become proactive in reproducing garden communities of the Kingdom wherever we are and wherever we go in the future. That is our calling and our assignment from the One who commanded us to *"go and make disciples of* all nations, baptizing them in the name of the Father and of the Son and of the Holy Spirit, and teaching them to obey everything I have commanded you..." (Matt. 28:19-20a).

THE KINGDOM WE'VE ALL BEEN LOOKING FOR

Human history is replete with examples of good kings and bad kings, good kingdoms and bad kingdoms, benevolent governments and oppressive governments. One fact that stands out clearly is this: As the king goes, so goes the kingdom. Since a kingdom is tied so closely to the nature and character of its king, it is virtually impossible for a good kingdom to come from a bad king, or a bad kingdom to come from a good king. Jesus put it this way:

> *No good tree bears bad fruit, nor does a bad tree bear good fruit. Each tree is recognized by its own fruit. People do not pick figs from thornbushes, or grapes from briers. The good man brings good things out of the good stored up in his heart, and the evil man brings evil things out of the evil stored up in his heart. For out of the overflow of his heart his mouth speak"* (Luke 6:43-45).

Fortunately for all of us, the King of kings is a good King, and His Kingdom is a good kingdom. That is why we who are citizens of the Kingdom of Heaven can live and work for the Kingdom—and engage the popular culture with it—in complete confidence that we are serving not only God, but also the better interests of our fellow humans who are not yet in the Kingdom. Our King's rule is just and righteous. He rules with fairness, grace, compassion, mercy, and, most of all, love. And in His love He delights to give all good things to His children, His people. James, the brother of Jesus, wrote, *"Every good and perfect gift is from above, coming down from the Father of the heavenly lights, who does not change like shifting shadows"* (James 1:17). Jesus Himself said, *"Do not be afraid, little flock, for your Father has been pleased to give you the kingdom"* (Luke 12:32). No matter who we are, and whether we realize it or not, the Kingdom of Heaven is the kingdom we have always been looking for.

The nature of a king and his government determines the quality of life in his kingdom. If the king is corrupt, then his kingdom will be characterized by corruption, oppression, evil, and injustice. Such was the experience of millions, including the early Christians, under the rule of Rome. The Roman Empire endured a succession of evil and depraved rulers, and the quality of life across the empire reflected it. The King of the Ages, however, rules with absolute love, beneficence, and equanimity.

In addition, the wealth of a kingdom will be reflected in the lifestyle of its people. If the kingdom is rich and the king is good, the people will be well off. If the kingdom is poor, or the king corrupt, the people will live in poverty. Our Kingdom belongs to a King who owns everything. The Earth is the Lord's, and everything on it (see Ps. 24:1), and the heavens belong to Him as well (see Ps. 115:16). He bestows favor and honor and withholds no good thing from those who obey Him (see Ps. 84:11). And the apostle Paul assures us that *"God will meet all your needs according to His glorious riches in Christ Jesus"* (Phil. 4:19). He will supply everything we need on Earth, but not necessarily from the Earth. His supply will come to us from the limitless riches of Heaven.

In other words, our needs can be met based on how much the Kingdom has. Unlimited resources mean unlimited provision. There is no lack in the Kingdom of Heaven. The meaning of Matthew 6:33 is that if we place our top priority on seeking first the Kingdom and righteousness of God, then His government will supply all of our basic necessities as a Kingdom obligation to its citizens. But the King fulfills this obligation freely and willingly out of His love for us.

Finally, the quality of life of citizens of a kingdom is at the mercy of the character of the king. Jesus said,

> *"Come to Me, all you who are weary and burdened, and I will give you rest. Take My yoke upon you and learn from Me, for I am gentle and humble in heart, and you will find rest for your souls. For My yoke is easy and My burden is light"* (Matthew 11:28-30).

"All" means everybody. The King has the power to give rest to everyone who comes to Him—including all 7 billion plus of us on the face of the Earth. This is not some sweet and sentimental religious statement; it is a legal Kingdom decree. "Come to Me, all 7 billion and more of you; I can heal you all, house you all, feed you all, dress you all, and bless you all—and still have as many resources as when I began."

Jesus is a good King, and His Kingdom is just what the world needs, which is why He wants to fill the Earth with His Kingdom communities and use His citizens to do it.

VICTORY THROUGH SERVICE

But how do we do it? What is our personal strategy for carrying out our King's Garden Expansion Program? We must not use the methods or ways of the world because the world's ways are at odds with the ways of the Kingdom. The world operates through self-promotion and the pursuit of selfish ambition. But the Kingdom operates by different principles. An incident involving two of Jesus' disciples gave Him the opportunity to teach all of them about greatness and advancement in the Kingdom of Heaven:

Then the mother of Zebedee's sons [James and John] *came to Jesus with her sons and, kneeling down, asked a favor of Him.*

"What is it you want?" He asked.

She said, "Grant that one of these two sons of mine may sit at Your right and the other at Your left in Your kingdom."

"You don't know what you are asking," Jesus said to them. "Can you drink the cup I am going to drink?"

"We can," they answered.

Jesus said to them, "You will indeed drink from My cup, but to sit at My right or left is not for Me to grant. These places belong to those for whom they have been prepared by My Father."

When the ten heard about this, they were indignant with the two brothers. Jesus called them together and said, "You know that the rulers of the Gentiles lord it over them, and their high officials exercise authority over them. Not so with you. Instead, whoever wants to become great among you must be your servant, and whoever wants to be first must be your slave—just as the Son of Man did not come to be served, but to serve, and to give His life as a ransom for many" (Matthew 20:20-28).

"Not so with you." With these words Jesus clearly and permanently distinguished Kingdom life and ways from those of the world. In the world, kings and rulers vaunt their authority over others. "Not so with you." In the world, officials and others in power exercise authority over others, often in selfish or oppressive ways. "Not so with you." In the world, people put themselves forward, scrambling over or pulling down anyone who gets in their way in their struggle to become top dog. "Not so with you."

Greatness and success in the Kingdom come not through self-promotion and ambitious positioning, but through self-abasement and servanthood. By self-abasement I do not mean false modesty or humility, or becoming a pushover or a doormat for people to walk all over. Self-abasement means a genuinely humble spirit that regards selfless service to others in the name of the King as the greatest honor and privilege that anyone could be given. As sinners who were once in rebellion against God, we deserve nothing from Him except judgment and condemnation. Yet God, in His great mercy and love, forgave our sins through Christ, brought us into His glorious and eternal Kingdom, and assigned us to represent His Kingdom on Earth, even as we enjoy all its benefits. What greater privilege could there be?

"Not so with you." Our culture is different. We don't do things the way the rest of the world does. In the world, people seek greatness through money, power, and the praise and admiration of others. Jesus said that they have their reward (see Matt. 6:2). Greatness in the Kingdom of God comes through service, the selfless giving of ourselves for the benefit of others. If our King came to serve rather than to be served, how can we do anything different?

FIND YOUR GIFT AND SERVE IT TO THE WORLD

"The Son of Man did not come to be served, but to serve, and to give His life as a ransom for many" (Matt. 20:28). Notice the progression here: Jesus became a servant, and then He gave Himself. By His example He is telling us: "Find your gift and serve it to the world. That is how you will infect people with the Kingdom." If you set your heart on the Kingdom of Heaven and your sights on serving others in the King's name, He will open doors of opportunity for you that would never open otherwise. He will take you to places you would never be able to go on your own and enable you to impact lives you would never even come close to touching any other way. He will take you to personal heights of joy, prosperity, and contentment beyond your wildest dreams and give you a broader influence in your world than you have ever imagined. But those things come not by seeking them, but by seeking Him; not by seeking the gifts, but by seeking the Giver.

Jesus said that *whoever* wants to become great in the Kingdom must become a servant. "Whoever" means that greatness in the Kingdom is available to anyone—anyone willing to pay the price, that is. And what is the price? It is setting aside your own will and ambitions and offering yourself willingly as a servant—even a slave—of the King. It is giving up your right to yourself in complete surrender to the will and purpose of God, to go where He says to go and to do what He says to do.

Everyone dreams of being great, and there is nothing evil in that desire. We all want to be part of something significant. This is perfectly natural. Such a desire comes from God, because He created us for greatness, but we lost it when we lost the Kingdom. We can get it back, but not by walking on top of people, pushing people down, lording it over people, conniving, scheming, lying, stealing, or dealing under the table. Those are the ways of the world. In God's country, if you want to be great, you first must become the servant of all.

What Jesus was actually saying is that when we become servants of the King, we are supposed to serve something to the world. If we want to become great, we have to find our gift, refine it, and serve it to the world, not for our sake but for the world's, and for the sake of our King and His great name.

There is actually a process. First, you must find your gift; discover it. Second, you must define your gift; understand it. Third, you must refine your gift; begin using it in small ways faithfully, and in larger ways as the Lord gives you opportunity. This means distributing your gift for free, giving it away. Slaves don't receive pay for their labors; they work for free. But as you serve humbly and faithfully, giving freely of yourself, the King will be watching and will reward you. As you prove yourself faithful in little things, He will entrust you with greater things.

So keep on laboring faithfully in the men's ministry, or the children's ministry, or the music ministry, or the soup kitchen, or wherever God has placed you and however He has gifted you. Set your heart on the Kingdom, serve your gift to the world, and be faithful; and eventually God will elevate you in some way. You have to become a slave of your gift, for when you serve your gift, you are serving yourself to others. And the more you give of yourself, the greater you will become in the eyes of those you serve, because they will see in you the image, likeness, and heart of the King.

God's big idea was to extend His kingly influence and culture from the celestial to the terrestrial by planting garden communities throughout the Earth that would perfectly reflect the richness and abundant life of His heavenly Kingdom. And He chose to do it through citizen-servants like you and me who will seek first His Kingdom and His righteousness and live exclusively for Him. We do this by humbling ourselves and giving ourselves freely to others so that they may see Him in us, learn of His Kingdom from us, and apply for citizenship themselves. Let us be faithful to our calling and hasten the day when *"the earth will be filled with the knowledge of the glory of the Lord, as the waters cover the sea"* (Hab. 2:14).

■ ■ ■ ■ ■ ■ ■ ■ ■ ■ ■ ■ ■ ■ ■ ■ ■ ■ ■

Part II

40 DAYS TO DISCOVERING GOD'S
BIG IDEA FOR YOUR LIFE

■ ■ ■ ■ ■ ■ ■ ■ ■ ■ ■ ■ ■ ■ ■ ■ ■ ■ ■

THIS devotional journal is a continuation of the concepts and principles presented in *Reclaiming God's Original Purpose for Your Life*. God's idea originated in the mind and heart of the Creator and was the motivation and purpose for the creation of the physical universe and the human species. His idea is superior to all the collective wisdom and ideas of human intellect. It is an idea that is beyond the philosophical reserves of human history and supersedes the institutions that have governed humankind since his first human society.

This 40-day devotional journal is designed to help you discover how "God's Big Idea" includes you. God wants to make the Earth a place of Kingdom harmony and peace and He would like you to be a part of His plan.

Each day is divided into four inspiring and thought-provoking sections:

Scripture—relevant and life-changing words from God.

Devotion—excerpts from *Reclaiming God's Original Purpose for Your Life*.

Considerations—questions and ideas for thoughtful pause.

Meditation—thoughts that prompt introspection and action.

Each day will bring you closer to discovering God's love and plan for you, including: how to fulfill your destiny now; how to enjoy continuous fellowship with the Lord; how to turn the Earth into a place filled with His culture; and how you can make a positive difference in what happens on Earth.

You will experience for yourself through personal devotion and journaling how to be directly involved in "God's Big Idea" by helping to plant and multiply His garden communities where all God's children live fruitful and abundant lives.

GOD'S KINGDOM ON EARTH

God blessed them and said to them, "Be fruitful and increase in number; fill the earth and subdue it. Rule over the fish of the sea and the birds of the air and over every living creature that moves on the ground" (Genesis 1:28).

TODAY'S DEVOTION

RELIGION is man's idea, not God's.

God's original idea is much bigger and much better than anything we humans could ever dream up. And what was God's big idea? He decided to extend His heavenly Kingdom to the earthly plane, to expand His supernatural realm into the natural realm. Or, to put it another way, God decided to fill the Earth with the culture of Heaven.

How did God bring His big idea into being? In this, as in almost everything else He does, God did the unexpected. Typically, human kingdoms and empires rise—and fall—through war and conquest. Not God's. Because His thoughts are not our thoughts and His ways are not our ways (see Isa. 55:8), God did something completely different. When God decided to bring the culture of Heaven to Earth He did not use war. He did not use conquest. He did not issue a code of laws. No, when God set out to bring Heaven to Earth, He did something much simpler, something uniquely beautiful and wonderful.

He planted a garden.

(Chapter One)

CONSIDERATIONS

1. Can you think of three earthly kingdoms that have risen and fallen? Name them and the reason for their ultimate demise.

2. In what ways has religion failed humankind?

3. What is the "alternate government" that will change the world?

4. Because many cultural conflicts are religiously based, what can be done to help solve the differences in ideologies?

5. How can you personally tap into God's big idea to help change your world for the better?

MEDITATION

God initiated His Kingdom on earth by planting a Garden in Eden, a place specially prepared as the habitation for the first human representatives of His Kingdom government on earth. From this hub of abundance and beauty, they would follow their government's mandate to *"Be fruitful and multiply"* (Gen. 1:28 NKJV), filling the Earth with their kind and planting Kingdom "gardens" wherever they went. In this manner, like leaven in bread, they would infuse the territory of Earth with the nation of Heaven.

(Chapter One)

Are you willing to plant a garden in your neighborhood or your city?

What could your first step be?

GOD'S ORIGINAL INTENT

The heavens declare the glory of God; the skies proclaim the work of His hands (Psalm 19:1).

TODAY'S DEVOTION

INTENT can be defined as "original purpose." It is more important for us to know what a person intended than to know what he or she said. If we do not properly discern intent, misunderstanding will follow. This is one reason why there are so many confused people in the world. Because we have misunderstood God's original intent, we have misunderstood not only ourselves, but also God's purpose for us on earth.

Intent is also the most critical component of motivation. It is the source of motivation and the reason why someone does something or creates something. Unless specifically stated, however, intent is usually hidden. A good example of this is a work of art by a master painter. Artists rarely state their intents plainly; they let their art speak for itself. For those who take the time and effort to search it out, the intent behind an artist's work can be discerned from the painting itself. No other explanation is necessary.

(Chapter One)

CONSIDERATIONS

1. Do you agree that, "if intent is unknown, misunderstanding is inevitable"? Have your intentions ever been misunderstood by others? What was the result?

2. God's intentions are found in the Bible. Cite several Scripture passages that clearly reveal God's intent for your life.

3. Most religions focus on trying to get God's attention, which is the wrong approach. In what ways have you tried to get God's *attention*, instead of trying to discover His *intention*?

4. Have you had a special revelation from God that has brought you deeper understanding of His intent for your life or that of a loved one? Explain.

5. God speaks to you through His creation and His Word—list several ways in which you open your heart and mind to what He has to say to you.

MEDITATION

The phrase "God said" (see Gen. 1:26-28), indicates that what follows is the expression of the intent that God purposed beforehand in His mind. Whenever God speaks, we need to listen carefully, because we are about to receive His hidden intention. In this case, we learn God's intention—His purpose—in creating the universe, the planet we call Earth along with all its creatures, and especially, the human race.

(Chapter One)

Many times God's intentions are misunderstood—how does that affect our purpose and response to His voice?

Day 3

YOUR HOME BASE

Now the Lord God had planted a garden in the east, in Eden; and there He put the man He had formed. . . . The Lord God took the man and put him in the Garden of Eden to work it and take care of it (Genesis 2:8,15).

TODAY'S DEVOTION

GOD'S original intent was to colonize Earth with Heaven.

I understand that most people today think of colonization in very negative terms, particularly those who have lived under colonial rule, as I have. And with good reason: throughout history almost all of human colonization has been characterized by coercion, brutality, greed, exploitation, victimization, and oppression. These traits, in fact, reflect the nature and tactics of satan, the original enemy of humanity, who illegally seized control of God's original garden "colony," and deposed its rightful rulers, Adam and Eve.

Colonization was God's original idea, but His colony on Earth took the form of a garden. As an analogy, a garden shares the same general traits as a colony, but without all the negative baggage. In sharp contrast to the violent and forceful way human empires expand, God's way was much more subtle. Just as a garden gradually, beautifully, and completely transforms the fallow ground where it is planted, the influence of God's Kingdom on Earth grows gradually and often invisibly until eventually it will fill the earth, infusing it with the culture of Heaven.

(Chapter One)

CONSIDERATIONS

1. Jesus likened the process of Kingdom growth to the way yeast leavens bread (see Matt. 13:33). Are you experiencing a continual, gradual spiritual growth?

2. How does establishing Kingdom gardens fulfill His ultimate goal to fill the Earth with His glory?

3. When God created humankind He gave us rulership over the Earth, but He never gave us ownership. What is the difference between the two?

4. Is it possible for God's full glory to be manifested on the Earth? Why or why not?

5. Because Jesus' mission was to reestablish the Kingdom of Heaven on Earth, His first recorded public words were, *"Repent, for the kingdom of heaven is near"* (Matt. 4:17b). How do you think this message applies to His mission?

MEDITATION

As the initial outpost of God's invisible Kingdom in the visible realm, Eden was a touch of Heaven on Earth. Everything about it reflected Heaven's culture, government, and ways. Truly, it was paradise. Unfortunately, this idyllic state of affairs did not last long.

(Chapter One)

Establishing His glory within your personal garden is what He desires.

Is your home base in God's Kingdom on Earth? Why or why not?

HIS KINGDOM COME

Our Father in heaven, hallowed be Your name, Your kingdom come, Your will be done on earth as it is in heaven (Matthew 6:9-10).

TODAY'S DEVOTION

GOD'S big idea was to reproduce the Kingdom of Heaven in the visible realm by planting a Kingdom outpost on the Earth and populating it with Kingdom citizens who would govern according to Kingdom government, live according to Kingdom culture, and expand Kingdom influence until it filled and transformed the Earth. Politically speaking, the term for this kind of governmental expansion is *colonization*. As a Kingdom outpost on Earth, Eden was a *colony* of Heaven established by a righteous, just, and benevolent King who is *"compassionate and gracious, slow to anger, and abounding in love"* (see Ps. 103:8).

(Chapter One)

CONSIDERATIONS

1. List the four similarities between Heaven and Eden before the Fall.

2. Why did God create the Earth before creating Adam?

3. Why is it essential for a nation to share a common language?

4. Without laws, a constitution, and moral convictions, what does a nation consist of?

5. Common values bind a nation together—why?

MEDITATION

Planting a Kingdom Garden on Earth is still God's big idea—and His purpose for today. God is still in the horticultural business. All Kingdom citizens share a common call and commission from their King to be royal gardeners, sowing seeds and planting "gardens" of Kingdom culture and government throughout the world until *"the earth shall be filled with the knowledge of the glory of the Lord, as the waters cover the sea"* (Hab. 2:14 KJV).

(Chapter One)

Are you willing to become a royal gardener, or are you too comfortable with the way things are? What would change your mind?

WHY NOT EARLIER—
OR LATER?

But do not forget this one thing, dear friends: With the Lord a day is like a thousand years, and a thousand years are like a day. The Lord is not slow in keeping His promise, as some understand slowness (2 Peter 3:8-9).

TODAY'S DEVOTION

BETWEEN the time that Adam and Eve lost the earthly outpost of the Kingdom of Heaven to satan the pretender and the time Jesus Christ appeared announcing its restoration, thousands of years passed. Why did God wait so long before reestablishing His Kingdom on Earth? Why did He allow so much time to pass? Why was Christ born in the particular time in history in which He appeared? Why not earlier—or later?

In answering these questions, we must understand first of all that God views time and history differently than we humans do because He is bound by neither. From the perspective of eternity, God can take all the "time" He needs to accomplish His purposes.

(Chapter Two)

CONSIDERATIONS

1. Has the timing of circumstances and situations ever caused you to wonder if God's hand was holding the clock still?

2. List a few times when you thought something like, *Wow—that was perfect timing!*

3. How was Rome a model for God's plan for Kingdom expansion?

4. In what ways did Jesus legitimize Roman authority?

5. In what ways do you legitimize your national government's authority?

MEDITATION

God waited to send His Son to the Earth until an earthly kingdom appeared that looked, however imperfectly, like His own, so that when Jesus preached about the Kingdom, everyone would know what He was talking about. Christ came at the right time, into the right setting, the right culture, the right kingdom, and the right environment, because He was preaching exactly what was happening in the world under the Roman Empire.

(Chapter Two)

Are you sometimes frustrated with your earthly government?

What lessons can be learned from Jesus' example?

DO AS THE ROMANS DO

"Show Me the coin used for paying the tax." They brought Him a denarius, and He asked them, "Whose portrait is this? And whose inscription?"

"Caesar's," they replied.

Then He said to them, "Give to Caesar what is Caesar's, and to God what is God's."

When they heard this, they were amazed. So they left Him and went away (Matthew 22:19-22).

TODAY'S DEVOTION

ANOTHER way Jesus acknowledged the legitimacy of the Roman form of government is the fact that He used a portion of that form as a model for establishing His own government on earth—His church.

Whenever the Romans set up their government in a new territory, they sent a *procurator*, or governor, to rule the province in the name and authority of the emperor. At the time of Jesus' public ministry, Pontius Pilate was the procurator of Judea. In addition, the Romans borrowed many ideas of government from the Greeks, modified them, and made them their own. One of these was the idea of a "called-out" assembly of citizens who met democratically over matters of common concern. Both the word and the concept would have been familiar to the people of Jesus' day: the concept, because they saw it in action regularly in everyday government; and the word, because of its frequent appearance in the *Septuagint*, the Greek translation of the Old Testament in common use in Jesus' day, which referred specifically to the children of God using the word *ekklesia*.

(Chapter Two)

CONSIDERATIONS

1. In what way is the Church, Christ's Body on Earth, a governmental body rather than a religious body?

2. Is Jesus a religious leader or a government agent on a Kingdom mission? How does this concept change your perspective about Him?

3. Contrary to popular belief, the Great Commission is not a religious statement, but a declaration of government policy. As a Kingdom government appointee, how will you carry out this responsibility?

4. The Church Jesus established is not a religious institution but a governmental agency charged with publicizing and implementing Kingdom principles and policies throughout the Earth. In your opinion, how have His appointees succeeded...or failed?

5. List a few ways in which the deceiver distorts the Kingdom government's role and responsibilities.

MEDITATION

All authority in heaven and on earth has been given to Me. Therefore go and make disciples of all nations, baptizing them in the name of the Father and of the Son and of the Holy Spirit, and teaching them to obey everything I have commanded you. And surely I will be with you always, to the very end of the age (Matthew 28:18-20).

(Chapter Two)

How does this Scripture passage speak to your heart? To your mind? To your spirit?

Day 7

GOOD SEED AND BAD SEED

The one who sowed the good seed is the Son of Man. The field is the world, and the good seed stands for the sons of the kingdom. The weeds are the sons of the evil one, and the enemy who sows them is the devil. The harvest is the end of the age, and the harvesters are angels (Matthew 13:37-40).

TODAY'S DEVOTION

THERE are two kinds of people in the world: those who are children of the Kingdom of Heaven, and those who are not. Christ Himself made this distinction clear in a teaching story He told about a farmer who planted good seed in his field. At night an enemy came and planted weeds in the midst of the wheat. No one was the wiser until the wheat and the weeds sprouted up together. The farmer told his workers not to pull up the weeds for danger of uprooting the wheat as well. Instead, he allowed both to grow until harvest time, when the weeds were gathered and burned, but the wheat was stored in the granary (see Matt. 13:24-30).

(Chapter Two)

CONSIDERATIONS

I. Contrast the aspects of God's Kingdom of Heaven and the pretender's false kingdom. (Example: joy vs. fear)

2. Why is it that most religions, including Christianity, focus on preparing people to leave Earth rather than to plant roots and "stick around for a while"?

3. Do you believe you have been given the ability to make a positive difference in your realm of influence?

4. Are the weeds in your garden choking out the beauty of the seeds sown by the Master Gardener? Will you be willing to burn the weeds at harvest time?

5. When others look at the fruit of your life, can they see evidence of good seeds? List a few of the seeds that you've been blessed to produce.

MEDITATION

As with many of His other stories, Jesus used a garden-like analogy in Matthew 13:37-43a to talk about the Kingdom of Heaven. And while the overall meaning of the story relates to the end of this present age, one thing that stands out clearly is the existence in the world of two distinct cultures: Kingdom culture and the culture of the "evil one," the pretender. Just as wheat and weeds are easy to tell apart, so too is Kingdom culture distinct from worldly culture.

Our lives should leave absolutely no doubt as to which culture we live under.

(Chapter Two)

Are you a royal Kingdom citizen or a slave in the evil one's culture?

Day 8

THE POWER OF
THE GARDEN PRINCIPLE

And a highway will be there; it will be called the Way of Holiness. The unclean will not journey on it; it will be for those who walk in that Way; wicked fools will not go about on it. No lion will be there, nor will any ferocious beast get up on it; they will not be found there. But only the redeemed will walk there, and the ransomed of the Lord will return. They will enter Zion with singing; everlasting joy will crown their heads. Gladness and joy will overtake them, and sorrow and sighing will flee away (Isaiah 35:8-10).

TODAY'S DEVOTION

EVERYONE in the world is looking for the Kingdom of Heaven, even though most of them don't realize it. People are not looking for religion. Buddhism does not satisfy. Hinduism does not satisfy. Islam does not satisfy. Judaism does not satisfy. "Religious" Christianity does not satisfy. Money and material riches do not satisfy. We were created to rule a garden domain, and we will never be content outside that environment. The King's garden expansion program is designed to draw many people into His Kingdom from all over the world and prepare them for Kingdom life and leadership in the *"new heaven and...new earth"* (Rev. 21:1) that He is already preparing.

(Chapter Two)

CONSIDERATIONS

1. Life under the pretender's evil rule is characterized by greed, selfishness, hatred, violence, war, murder, envy, strife, lust, immorality, cruelty, brutality, empty religion, and oppression. List the characteristics of life in God's Kingdom:

2. Jesus preached a simple, pure message. Modeled after His, write your own mission statement.

3. The power to walk in authority comes from God. What steps can you take to avail yourself of His power?

4. Jesus imparted His power and authority to His disciples, and they healed the sick and spread the Gospel. In what other ways were the disciples empowered?

5. The power of the Garden Principle is irresistible, because it is the power of the King, the Master Gardener. That same power lies within the hearts and lives of every Kingdom citizen—is it powerful enough to spread the Gospel worldwide?

MEDITATION

Jesus Christ came to Earth to reclaim the desert and transform it once more into a great garden, the vibrant life and abundance of which reflect the character, nature, and environment of His Father's heavenly Kingdom. (See Isaiah 35:1-10.) He was an oasis—a garden in the desert—and He planted seeds of life, righteousness, and holiness that sprouted into other oases.

(Chapter Two)

Are you an oasis in the middle of the world in which you live?

Day 9

HE IS IN CONTROL

For the foundations of the earth are the Lord's; upon them He has set the world (I Samuel 2:8).

TODAY'S DEVOTION

NOT long after national elections in the Bahamas, someone asked me in an airport, "What do you think about your new government?"

I replied, "I only have one government."

It doesn't matter who occupies the prime minister's chair or the Speaker of Parliament's chair or the governor's mansion; it doesn't matter who sits on the throne and is called king or queen. There is only one government, and it belongs to Him whose throne will never move or be toppled: Almighty God, the King of kings and Lord of lords. His rule in Heaven is eternal, without beginning or end. But He also created the Earth and established His Kingdom there as well.

(Chapter Three)

CONSIDERATIONS

I. The words *earth* and *world* are often used interchangeably, but they refer to two different things in First Samuel 2:8b, "*For the foundations of the earth are the Lord's; upon them He has set the world."* Describe the difference.

2. God rules directly in Heaven, but His plan for the Earth was to rule it indirectly through human representatives created in His own image. What were Adam and Eve's responsibilities?

3. In Romans 13:1-5, Paul makes it clear that God is the true authority behind human affairs. Can you name a few modern-day countries in which the government leaders defy the rule of God?

4. It is easy to think that satan is in control of some governments, but Scripture tells us differently. List four or five verses that declare the sovereignty of God in world affairs.

5. Write Isaiah 45:22-23 in your own words and explain what it means to you.

MEDITATION

Satan the pretender may believe that he runs the show and controls the governments of the Earth, but it is the King of Heaven who guides human history and destiny toward His desired ends. He raises up one power and brings down another, all in accordance with His sovereign will and purpose.

(Chapter Three)

Day 10

EARTH'S ONLY
LEGITIMATE CULTURE

*As the king was walking on the roof of the royal palace of Babylon, he said,
"Is not this the great Babylon I have built as the royal residence, by my mighty
power and for the glory of my majesty?"*

*The words were still on his lips when a voice came from heaven, "This is what
is decreed for you, King Nebuchadnezzar: Your royal authority has been taken
from you. You will be driven away from people and will live with the wild
animals; you will eat grass like cattle. Seven times will pass by for you until
you acknowledge that the Most High is sovereign over the kingdoms of men
and gives them to anyone He wishes." Immediately what had been said about
Nebuchadnezzar was fulfilled. . . (Daniel 4:29-33).*

TODAY'S DEVOTION

HUMAN empires rise and fall, but the Kingdom of God stands forever.
Earthly rulers who forget or refuse to acknowledge the One to whom
they are accountable set themselves up for judgment, and even destruction.
Nebuchadnezzar, king of Babylon, ruled the mightiest empire the world had
ever known up to that time, but even he had to learn to humble himself before
the God of Heaven.

(Chapter Three)

CONSIDERATIONS

1. What caused the ultimate downfall of Nebuchadnezzar? Are there government leaders today who are guilty of this same attitude?

2. Many earthly governments are in disorder. This can be attributed to what principle?

3. Human-based culture is illegitimate and rooted in evil and destruction. What can be done to help them recognize the legitimate Kingdom of God?

4. The clash between the illegitimate and legitimate cultures is continually felt worldwide, especially recently, with the rise of terrorism, which is often based on religious convictions. Are there ways you can make changes within your realm of influence?

5. Name other culture clashes we are faced with today, and describe how worldly governments have contributed to the legitimization of perversion.

MEDITATION

The shrinking of our global community through telecommunications technology and the Internet has greatly accelerated the rate and intensity of culture clash. A "take-no-prisoners" war is being waged for the soul of our culture, and it is vitally important that we identify the nature of the fight. What do we do when we discover that mosques are popping up next to churches all over America, or when the need to preserve democratic freedom and individual rights conflicts with the need for greater security?

What do we do when the counterculture of sexual perversion labors and lobbies vigorously to dignify and legitimize itself through legislation? How should we respond to the claim that two men or two women should be able to marry each other, and to raise children in such a same-gender household? This is no time to play religious games; the very life of our culture is at stake. We need help from beyond ourselves—help from the Creator of the Earth's original and only legitimate culture.

(Chapter Three)

How have the culture clashes affected your life, your worldview?

Day 11

CULTURE POWER

Do not conform any longer to the pattern of this world, but be transformed by the renewing of your mind. Then you will be able to test and approve what God's will is—His good, pleasing, and perfect will (Romans 12:2).

TODAY'S DEVOTION

CULTURE is stronger than politics. It really doesn't matter who is in power. Politicians come and go, and governments rise and fall, but culture still remains. Culture is also more powerful than religion. One of the biggest challenges that Church leaders faced during the first few centuries of the Church's existence was how to keep those who were coming into the Church out of pagan backgrounds from bringing elements of their pagan culture with them and blending these with their new faith in Christ. Even today we continue to see the enormous power of culture in the fact that many believers and Kingdom citizens display lifestyles that differ little from those of people who make no claim to be in the Kingdom.

The United States of America has a rich historical heritage of faith and even today has the highest percentage of citizens who claim to be believers (Christians) of any of the industrialized nations. Yet every year in America, 500,000 unborn babies are aborted—*legally.*

(Chapter Three)

CONSIDERATIONS

1. The enormous power of culture affects many believers and Kingdom citizens who display lifestyles that differ little from those who make no claim to be in the Kingdom. Why?

2. The power of culture trumps religion in its ability to shape the thoughts, values, and beliefs of people, and to influence their behavior and what they are willing to accept. How can impotent religion be replaced with empowering Kingdom authority?

3. How and why has homosexuality become a cultural norm in a country that professes to have more believers than any other industrialized nation?

4. Why did God think it was necessary to change the minds of the Israelites through presenting them with a set of commandments?

5. How can reading—or not reading—the Bible change the culture of a nation?

MEDITATION

Culture is the manifestation of the collective thinking of a people. This means that whoever controls the minds of the people creates and controls the culture. Culture is also a product of law. The most effective way to change a culture is to control its laws, because whatever is instated into law eventually will become accepted as "normal" by most citizens, regardless of how they might have felt at the beginning. This is all part of the process of mind control.

(Chapter Three)

Are there laws you don't agree with? Is there a way to change them? Have you ever thought of getting involved in the political process as a way to control culture?

Day 12

DECLARATION OF INDEPENDENCE

The God who made the world and everything in it is the Lord of heaven and earth and does not live in temples built by hands (Acts 17:24).

TODAY'S DEVOTION

CULTURE rests on the foundation of law. God's laws are not meant to restrict us, but to protect us and to ensure that His culture fills the Earth. This is what Adam and Eve forgot when they chose to rebel against the King in Eden. When they ate of the one tree in the Garden that God had placed off-limits, they did more than commit personal sins for the sake of pleasure and enlightenment; theirs was an act of treason against the government of their Creator. Their disobedience was, in fact, a declaration of independence from God and His righteous, loving, and benevolent rule. Adam and Eve turned their backs on God's Kingdom in favor of setting up a regime of their own making. Unfortunately, satan the pretender illegally seized the throne, began pulling the strings, and imposed his own culture of hatred, murder, and deceit.

(Chapter Three)

CONSIDERATIONS

1. God issued laws for us to obey in His Kingdom, which produce a community lifestyle that in turn creates a totally unique society. How does accepting His laws enhance your life?

2. Why is it that some cultures can coexist and others can only clash?

3. It was never God's desire or intent that there be a British culture, or an American culture, or a Bahamian culture. He wanted a Kingdom culture, one culture throughout the entire created realm. Do you believe this will happen in your lifetime? Why or why not?

4. When Adam and Eve declared their independence from God's law, what was the ultimate result? Who benefited?

5. List three things that the evil pretender steals from those who are under his rule.

MEDITATION

The Kingdom of Heaven is not about escaping Earth; it is about occupying the planet. As Kingdom citizens, we are destined to change this world. In the name of Jesus the King, nations and peoples will be set free from the cruel bondage and deadly culture of satan the pretender. The time of the Kingdom of God is upon us. Let His Kingdom come. Let His will be done on Earth as it is in Heaven. Let us live according to His laws and principles. Let His culture reign supreme. Let the Earth be filled with His glory.

(Chapter Three)

Are you prepared to declare independence from the corrupted world and accept your role as a Kingdom citizen?

Day 13

THE MASTER GARDENER

In the beginning was the Word, and the Word was with God, and the Word was God. He was with God in the beginning. Through Him all things were made; without Him nothing was made that has been made (John 1:1-3).

TODAY'S DEVOTION

ALTHOUGH John's reference to *"the Word"* through whom *"all things were made"* refers to Jesus Christ, the Son of God, the Spirit of God is also the Spirit of Christ, because they are all of one essence—one God in three Persons. By right and agency of creation, the Holy Spirit was the Master Gardener of Eden, the Governor of God's original colony on Earth. Like human colonial governors, He guides and oversees the lives and welfare of His citizens. Unlike His human counterparts, however, who live in fancy houses and mansions made with human hands, the Governor of the Kingdom lives in the hearts and lives of His citizens. As He was in Eden, He is still the Master Gardener, overseeing the planting, growth, fruitfulness, and reproduction of Kingdom "gardens" in the lives of Kingdom citizens and throughout the world.

(Chapter Four)

CONSIDERATIONS

I. A well-cared-for garden signals the presence of life in its fullest abundance, vitality, and beauty. What are some ways a garden can become unattractive or dead-looking?

2. The Master Gardener of Eden was present and intimately involved in its creation. He placed caretakers in the Garden to help tend to it. When they were banished for disobedience, what happened to the Garden?

3. Do you yearn to live in the midst of a beautiful garden created by the Master Gardener? How can you make this happen today?

4. What can you learn from the Master Gardener, the Holy Spirit, about tending to your personal garden of colorful bounty?

5. By right and agency of creation, the Holy Spirit was the Master Gardener of Eden, the Governor of God's original colony on Earth who guides and oversees the lives and welfare of His citizens. Have you accepted His guidance with thankfulness?

MEDITATION

The Islands of the Bahamas are the home of many beautiful gardens, both public and private. Most of us Bahamians take great pride in doing everything possible to make our nation a true island paradise of botanical richness and splendor. Of course, the same is true in many other parts of the world. There is something about a garden that stirs an inner chord in the spirit of most of us, a chord of peace, harmony...and *rightness*, as if to say, "This is the way nature is supposed to be." And of course, that is true.

(Chapter Four)

What other things stir your inner chord of peace, harmony, and rightness?

CARRYING OUT
THE KING'S WILL

Your kingdom come, Your will be done on earth as it is in heaven (Matthew 6:10).

TODAY'S DEVOTION

CARRYING out the will of the king is the paramount responsibility of the governor. The big difference between a king and a prime minister or president is that the latter two cannot always have their will or way in the country. They have to negotiate with Parliament or Congress. They have to debate and discuss and often make compromises just to get part of what they want. Even then, the final legislation is subject to judicial review and can be overturned if it is judged to violate the Constitution.

(Chapter Four)

CONSIDERATIONS

1. God is a God of government, not anarchy. In His orderly assembly of creation, God established His rule of law. How has that rule been distorted by the pretender?

2. What can believers do to restore the Master Gardener's government?

3. Proverbs 29:18 says, *"Where there is no revelation, the people cast off restraint; but blessed is he who keeps the law."* List a few areas where you have witnessed people casting off restraint.

4. God appointed a Governor, the Holy Spirit, to oversee the overall Garden Expansion Program. Are believers aware of their responsibility to carry out the will of the King through the prompting of the Governor?

5. A kingdom is not a democratic system—in a kingdom, the king's word is law and his will is absolute. Does our twenty-first century mindset of independence keep us from submitting to our King's authority?

MEDITATION

The Bible is about a King, His Kingdom, and His royal family. It is a royal document chronicling the purposes, desires, and decrees of the King, as well as the activities, past history, and future destiny of His children and heirs. It also describes the King's expansion program—His plan to expand His heavenly realm into earthly territory.

(Chapter Four)

How does the concept of being a royal heir conflict or mesh with your concept of being an independent individual?

OUR GOVERNOR, THE HOLY SPIRIT

In the same way, the Spirit helps us in our weakness. We do not know what we ought to pray for, but the Spirit Himself intercedes for us with groans that words cannot express. And He who searches our hearts knows the mind of the Spirit, because the Spirit intercedes for the saints in accordance with God's will (Romans 8:26-27).

TODAY'S DEVOTION

GOVERNORS in a kingdom are personal appointees of the king. They may be personal friends of the king, or at least known to him by reputation or recommendation. Either way, they are chosen for their loyalty to the king and their commitment to his policies. His purpose is their purpose, and his objectives, their objectives. Quite often they come from the very center of the royal court, intimates of the king who understand his thoughts and are of one mind with him.

This certainly describes the Holy Spirit, who never speaks of His own accord, but only that which He receives from God the Father, the King of Heaven. He is perfectly suited to be Governor of Heaven's Kingdom gardens on Earth because He knows perfectly the heart and mind of the King. This intimacy enables Him to conform the hearts and minds of Kingdom citizens to

those of the King, thus shaping the "gardens" of their lives to faithfully manifest the government and culture of Heaven.

(Chapter Four)

CONSIDERATIONS

1. The better you know a person, the more you can understand the
    person's motivations and temperament. How well do you know the
    Governor who was sent to counsel and comfort you?

2. The intimacy that the Governor has with the King enables Him to
    conform the hearts and minds of Kingdom citizens to those of the
    King. How does this relationship shape the gardens of their lives to
    faithfully manifest the government and culture of Heaven?

3. Because the Governor always carries out the will of the King, His
    presence in us enables us to do the same. In what ways can believers
    reflect the heart, nature, and character of our King?

4. A governor represents the authority of a king. Why do you think
    many people, both inside and outside the Kingdom, are confused
    about who the Holy Spirit is and what He does?

5. What the Spirit says will always be in agreement with what the
    Father and the Son say, and with what the Bible, the written Word of
    God, says. When contradictions are preached, do you immediately
    go to the Governor for clarification?

MEDITATION

As Governor of the Kingdom, the Holy Spirit is the official, designated
representative through whom all information from and about the King and His
Kingdom passes to His citizens. Because Jesus Christ is in Heaven seated at the

right hand of His Father (see Col. 3:1), it is impossible for us to receive any information from Christ, our King, except through the Holy Spirit. The Spirit is the one who guides us into all truth (see John 16:13), teaches us all things, and reminds us of everything Jesus taught us (see John 14:26). As long as the Governor is here, the King is here. As long as the Governor is here, the presence, power, and authority of the King are here. As long as the Governor is here, the Kingdom of Heaven is present on the Earth.

(Chapter Four)

Do you continually make yourself available for the Governor to speak to you? How can you be more open to receive His guidance?

FULFILLING HIS PROMISE

I tell you the truth, anyone who has faith in Me will do what I have been doing. He will do even greater things than these, because I am going to the Father (John 14:12).

TODAY'S DEVOTION

ALL of our talk about reproducing Kingdom gardens on Earth is simply another way of saying that God is in the process of recolonizing the planet with His Kingdom government and culture. This mission was so critical that He could entrust it to no one other than His Son, who alone possessed all the necessary qualifications. Jesus came into the world as a government agent on special assignment. Pilate, too, was a government official. This is why he understood Jesus' words when the religious leaders did not; he and Jesus were talking kingdom language.

By His own declaration, Jesus did nothing on His own, but only what He saw His Father doing (see John 5:19). And what did Jesus do? He healed the sick, made the lame walk, and gave sight to the blind, hearing to the deaf, and speech to the mute. He cast out demons and raised the dead. Jesus did all these things because He saw them first in the mind and heart of His Father. He knew these things were His Father's will, so He did them. The "colon" was clear. The border between countries was open, and the loving, merciful, compassionate, and healing will of the King passed from His supranatural realm into the realm of the natural.

(Chapter Four)

CONSIDERATIONS

1. The word "colony" comes from the Latin word *colonia*, which is transliterated into the Greek as *kolonia*. It comes from the verb *colere*, which literally means "to cultivate," as in planting and nurturing a garden. What does colonize mean to you in regard to planting Kingdom gardens?

2. What do *culture, agriculture,* and *horticulture* mean in relation to planting Kingdom gardens?

3. What connection did the Greeks make between the colon and the key to government?

4. When this connection is made from top to bottom, from Heaven to Earth, from the King to His citizens through the link of the Holy Spirit, what is the result?

5. The Governor, the Holy Spirit, wants to do the same things in and through us that Jesus did. Are most believers ready and willing to be His instruments of healing and power?

MEDITATION

The Holy Spirit came to dwell in us for the purpose of fulfilling the promise of John 14:12 in and through us. Christ is the Head, in Heaven, and we are His Body, on Earth. The Governor delivers the will of the Head to the Earth and carries it out through us, the Body. The Master Gardener takes the seeds and plans of the Owner and transfers the Garden of His supranatural realm into the natural world.

(Chapter Four)

How willing are you to become a useful, pliable, and available instrument for the Creator's plan?

Day 17

WHO IS TENDING
YOUR GARDEN?

No good tree bears bad fruit, nor does a bad tree bear good fruit. Each tree is recognized by its own fruit. People do not pick figs from thornbushes, or grapes from briers. The good man brings good things out of the good stored up in his heart, and the evil man brings evil things out of the evil stored up in his heart. For out of the overflow of his heart his mouth speaks. Why do you call Me, "Lord, Lord," and do not do what I say? (Luke 6:43-46)

TODAY'S DEVOTION

SUCCESSFUL gardens may have many caretakers, but they have only one master gardener, one person whose vision oversees the overall design. More than one guiding plan leads to confusion, inefficiency, inconsistent results, and stunted fruitfulness. This is precisely the dilemma many believers face. On the one hand, they claim to follow the King and to live according to His government, while on the other, they continue to listen to the desires of the pretender and fail or refuse to uproot the "weeds" of evil, rebellion, and destruction he has sown in their hearts. And then they wonder why their garden is choked off and produces little fruit.

(Chapter Five)

CONSIDERATIONS

1. If believers listen to the desires of the pretender and fail or refuse to uproot the "weeds" of evil, rebellion, and destruction he has sown in their hearts, what is the inevitable result?

2. Gardens are known by the consistency, quality, and abundance of the fruit they produce, and these are direct reflections of the skill and character of the gardener. If the garden is nonproducing, is this a reflection of the gardener as well?

3. The quality of the fruit depends on the nature of the root. In other words, the fruit we bear in our lives reveals who is tending our garden—the Master Gardener or the pretender. Who is tending your garden?

4. Just as the natural reflects the supernatural, the human race has mistreated the planet and misused its resources; this is a representation of the spiritual devastation wrought by the pretender's depraved rule. List a few examples of this mistreatment or misuse.

5. Every day we make choices that determine which fruit will manifest in our lives—either the bad fruit of the pretender or the good fruit of the Master Gardener. How easy is it for you to make the hard choices that produce the good fruit?

MEDITATION

The Bible is the record of God's plan to reclaim His earthly dominion and restore it to His original design and intent. As we have already seen, God's big idea from the beginning was to extend His heavenly Kingdom to Earth, and He chose to do it through His very own children. This was not a religious act, but an act of state. Adam and Eve had no religion in the Garden of Eden. What they did have was continuing fellowship with their Creator as they ruled the created order as His vice regents. In bringing Heaven to Earth, the King was simply enacting His own governmental policy. His purpose was to fill the Earth with His glory. He wanted to bring His own nature to the Earth, and that nature was reflected in the lush beauty, abundant fruitfulness, and absolute perfection of the Garden.

(Chapter Five)

Who is tending your garden?

SEEKING AND SAVING THE LOST

But Zacchaeus stood up and said to the Lord, "Look, Lord! Here and now I give half of my possessions to the poor, and if I have cheated anybody out of anything, I will pay back four times the amount." Jesus said to him, "Today salvation has come to this house, because this man, too, is a son of Abraham. For the Son of Man came to seek and to save what was lost" (Luke 19:8-10).

TODAY'S DEVOTION

IT was not God's purpose to leave Heaven and come to the Earth to rule it directly. He chose instead to give rulership of this domain to beings specially created for it. God created human beings specifically for the purpose of dominating the Earth for Him and filling it with His nature, character, and culture. No other created beings in Heaven or on Earth were suited for the task. Only humans were fit to rule the Earth because that is the way God designed us.

Unfortunately, in an act of treason and betrayal, the first two humans inadvertently surrendered their kingdom to one who greatly desired it but who was not qualified to rule it.

Jesus Christ, the King's Son, came to Earth to take it back. He came to regain what was lost. When Jesus announced the arrival of the Kingdom of

Heaven in Matthew 4:17, He was not bringing anything new to the Earth. He was bringing back what man had lost, and what the pretender had stolen.

(Chapter Five)

CONSIDERATIONS

1. What happened that resulted in a demonic pretender ascending the throne and the earthly realm declaring its independence from Heaven?

2. Zacchaeus was despised because of his unethical financial practices. How was his life changed after an encounter with Jesus? Compare Zacchaeus with a modern-day person fitting his description.

3. *"For the Son of Man came to seek and to save what was lost"* (Luke 19:10). Notice that Jesus said He came *"to seek and to save what was lost,"* rather than "who" was lost. Other versions of the Bible translate the phrase, *"that which was lost."* How do you explain this distinction?

4. In Luke 19:10, Jesus was referring also to the Kingdom of Heaven itself, which had been lost, and which He came to seek and to save. In what ways has the Kingdom been found and redeemed?

5. In what ways has the Kingdom remained lost and unredeemed?

MEDITATION

People everywhere are looking desperately for the Kingdom, even if they don't know it. This is why, when they encounter it—when they hear the message of the Kingdom—they, like Zacchaeus, find it irresistible. It is this attractive, magnetic quality of the Kingdom that Jesus had in mind when He said, *"From the days of John the Baptist until now, the kingdom of heaven has been forcefully advancing, and forceful men lay hold of it"* (Matt. 11:12). Once people know about the Kingdom and understand it, they flock to it, desperate to enter. This is only natural. The Kingdom is what we were created for.

(Chapter Five)

It is natural to want to be part of the Kingdom—why do some resist?

Day 19

SELF-GOVERNMENT
DISASTERS

*On the evening of that first day of the week, when the disciples were together,
with the doors locked for fear of the Jews, Jesus came and stood among them
and said, "Peace be with you!" After He said this, He showed them His hands
and side. The disciples were overjoyed when they saw the Lord.*

*Again Jesus said, "Peace be with you! As the Father has sent Me, I am sending
you." And with that He breathed on them and said, "Receive the Holy Spirit.
If you forgive anyone his sins, they are forgiven; if you do not forgive them,
they are not forgiven"* (John 20:19-23).

TODAY'S DEVOTION

WHEN Adam and Eve declared independence in the Garden by disobeying God's one restriction, they thought they could govern themselves and their earthly domain at least as well as God could, if not better. They
were wrong. No sooner had they "freed" themselves from God's control than
they found themselves deposed from their earthly thrones altogether. Their sin
against God corrupted their human nature, and they became enslaved to the
power and will of the pretender. He preferred to work behind the scenes, however, pulling the strings while letting them think they were governing themselves.

Humanity's efforts at self-government have been disastrous from the beginning. The first act of human self-government after leaving Eden was an act of fratricide: Cain murdered his brother Abel. And as a race, we humans have been chained by envy, hatred, and murder ever since.

(Chapter Five)

CONSIDERATIONS

1. Rather than bringing about self-improvement, all our efforts at self-government have moved us closer and closer to self-destruction. Why?

2. Thousands of wars and six millennia of social, scientific, and technological advancement have not changed things to any great degree. Why?

3. Jesus Christ inaugurated His public mission by announcing the return of the Kingdom and calling people to respond: *"Repent, for the kingdom of heaven is near"* (Matt. 4:17b). The word *repent* is seldom heard in today's political, religious, or other conversations. Why is there a need for an understanding of this concept?

4. For 33 years, from Jesus' birth to His ascension, the Holy Spirit showed up nowhere on the Earth except in Jesus Himself. Why are believers now worthy vessels for the indwelling of the Holy Spirit?

5. Through His death and resurrection, Jesus cleansed us of our sin—our rebellion against God—and gave us access to His Kingdom. Why is it so easy for believers to want to self-govern? What keeps us from submitting totally to His authority?

MEDITATION

[God] gave us the Governor to teach us how to live as Kingdom citizens. The Governor, the Holy Spirit, is the Master Gardener who ensures that the gardens of our lives produce good fruit that is appropriate and pleasing to the King, to whom the gardens belong. Could there be any greater freedom—or any greater destiny—than this?

(Chapter Five)

Is your independent nature stronger than your submissive nature? What can you do to surrender your idea and accept God's big idea?

ILLEGAL RESIDENT

In the same way, count yourselves dead to sin but alive to God in Christ Jesus. Therefore do not let sin reign in your mortal body so that you obey its evil desires. Do not offer the parts of your body to sin, as instruments of wickedness, but rather offer yourselves to God, as those who have been brought from death to life; and offer the parts of your body to Him as instruments of righteousness. For sin shall not be your master, because you are not under law, but under grace.

. . . You have been set free from sin and have become slaves to righteousness. . . .

But now that you have been set free from sin and have become slaves to God, the benefit you reap leads to holiness, and the result is eternal life. For the wages of sin is death, but the gift of God is eternal life in Christ Jesus our Lord (Romans 6:11-14,18,22-23).

TODAY'S DEVOTION

WE were created to be filled with the Spirit of God and to live in perfect harmony and fellowship with Him, not to be under the thumb of a demonic pretender who exercises illegitimate authority. This is why whenever Jesus encountered a demonic spirit possessing a human being, He cast out the spirit as an illegal resident. As believers, we have a choice as to who we allow to tend our gardens. One choice leads to a wasted and unfulfilled life, while the other leads to great abundance and fullness of life.

We have been trained by religion to be scared of the devil. Most of our churches have taught us to regard the world situation as hopeless, to prepare ourselves to leave, and then to pray for the Lord to rescue us out of this world. Having conceded victory to the pretender, we feel that all we can hope to do is circle the wagons and defend ourselves as best we can until Christ comes back and takes us away. We have become a bunch of holy sissies.

(Chapter Five)

CONSIDERATIONS

1. The devil wants to take up residence in us through demonic powers because he knows that once he is inside he can work through us to:

2. *"My prayer is not that You take them out of the world but that You protect them from the evil one"* (John 17:15). Why do you think Jesus felt it necessary to pray this prayer to God for us?

3. Why is it so hard for believers to realize that ultimately, satan the pretender poses no threat?

4. In league with our King, we have more power and authority than any fallen angel could ever hope to have. Is this the mindset of most believers? Why?

5. Our protection from the evil one is certain because of the King's love for us. List several times when you know your King saved you from danger, or forewarned you about a problem or situation.

MEDITATION

We are the legal rulers on Earth with the power, authority, and protection of our King behind us. Satan is a liar, usurper, and pretender, whose illegal power over us was broken forever at the Cross. Although we must always be on our guard against his schemes, deception, and treachery, as Kingdom citizens exercising our legitimate authority, we have no reason to fear him.

(Chapter Five)

Has the illegal resident taken up space in your community, school, house, heart?

Boot him out today!

Day 21

KINGDOM INFLUENCE

Once, having been asked by the Pharisees when the kingdom of God would come, Jesus replied, "The kingdom of God does not come with your careful observation, nor will people say, 'Here it is,' or 'There it is,' because the kingdom of God is within you" (Luke 17:20-21).

TODAY'S DEVOTION

BY now it should be abundantly clear that the Kingdom of Heaven is not a religion and has nothing at all to do with religion. In Eden, the original Kingdom Garden on Earth, there was no religion. There was no "worship" in the sense that we usually understand the word. Adam and Eve enjoyed full, open, and transparent fellowship and interaction with their Creator in a mutual relationship of pure love, with absolutely no guilt, shame, or fear. Their disobedience broke that relationship, and humanity's efforts to restore it on their own without divine assistance gave rise to religion.

The Kingdom of Heaven is the sovereign rulership of the King (God) over a territory (Earth). He impacts it with His will, purposes, and intent, producing a citizenry of people (*ekklesia*—the church) who express a culture reflecting His nature and lifestyle. Therefore, the Kingdom of Heaven is a real, literal country, although invisible to physical eyes because it is spiritual in nature. As King of Heaven, God's big idea was to extend the influence of His heavenly country over and throughout the Earth. So we are really talking about two things here: God's country and its influence.

(Chapter Six)

CONSIDERATIONS

1. Wherever the Kingdom of God is, the Kingdom of Heaven has influence. So wherever we go as Kingdom citizens, the influence of the King should go along. Are believers as aware as they should be about their sphere of influence?

2. A strong and rich culture can wield influence far beyond its geographical boundaries. Name a few ways culture or values have infiltrated nations outside their origin.

3. There are two kinds of influence: the influence of the moment, which spreads rapidly and then disappears just as quickly; and lasting influence, which grows more slowly, but succeeds through persistence and permeation. Give examples of how both types of influence can or cannot be of value to planting gardens for His glory.

4. What is meant by the term "irresistible influence" concerning the Kingdom?

5. At least 4,000 years have passed from the time Adam and Eve lost the Kingdom in Eden until Christ announced its return. God has been continually working out His plan. Do you see an end in sight?

MEDITATION

Ultimately, the influence of God's Kingdom is irresistible. This does not mean that everyone eventually will enter the Kingdom, but it does mean that someday everyone will acknowledge the reality, authority, and absolute supremacy of the Kingdom of Heaven. The apostle Paul stated plainly that the day will come when

> *at the name of Jesus every knee should bow, in heaven and on earth and under the earth, and every tongue confess that Jesus Christ is Lord, to the glory of God the Father* (Philippians 2:10-11).

The word *Lord* means "owner," and is a term properly applied to a king. Christ is the King of an eternal, all-powerful, all-knowing, omnipresent Kingdom, and one day everyone will confess that this is so, even those who have rejected His Kingdom.

(Chapter Six)

Is your influence making a difference in those around you? In those you love?

Day 22

EXPANDING YOUR INFLUENCE THROUGH PRAYER

...The kingdom of heaven is like a mustard seed, which a man took and planted in his field. Though it is the smallest of all your seeds, yet when it grows, it is the largest of garden plants and becomes a tree, so that the birds of the air come and perch in its branches (Matthew 13:31-32).

TODAY'S DEVOTION

ANYONE who spends any amount of time in the kitchen knows what yeast is and what it does (knowing *how* it does what it does is another matter). Yeast is one of the most powerful influencing agents in the world, and it exists for one reason: to infect whatever it is mixed into with its presence and influence. Jesus' comparison of the Kingdom of Heaven to yeast makes us think right away about impact.

While people caught up in religion think about leaving the Earth, Kingdom citizens focus on transforming it, the way yeast transforms a batch of dough. Yeast is not about giving up or giving in. It is about taking over. Yeast does not abandon dough; it affects it. Yeast never becomes dough. Instead, dough becomes what is called "yeast dough." Dough is weaker than yeast, and as the yeast works its way through, the dough gradually but irresistibly takes on new characteristics created by the yeast.

(Chapter Six)

CONSIDERATIONS

1. Yeast has not finished its job until it has "worked all through the dough." In the same way, Christ is not coming back to an Earth that is not "worked all through" with the influence of His Kingdom. Believers may feel frustrated because of an apparent lack of progress—but what does Christ say?

2. For many believers, prayer does not work the way it should because they have made it a religious exercise of pleading for a favor rather than a legal act of asserting their rights and privileges as Kingdom citizens. How do you view prayer? Is it working for you?

3. Becoming a Kingdom citizen through faith in Christ and the cleansing of our sins by His blood gives us complete access to these three gifts:

4. When we petition the King properly, we are asking for what He has already promised. According to Hebrews 4:16, we can approach the throne of grace with _____, so that we may receive _____ and find _____ to help in our time of need.

5. Write the Lord's Prayer and examine each word as you write. (See Matthew 6:9-13.)

MEDITATION

First, He says we must address our petition to the right Person: "*Our Father in heaven.*" God the Father is the King who is ruling in Heaven, and we are His citizens in His Garden outpost on Earth who are petitioning for an audience.

Second, we must pay proper respect when addressing the King: "*hallowed be Your name.*" To hallow God's name means to render utmost respect and reverence to His name, because His name is identified with His reputation. And because God is very jealous of His reputation, He is also jealous of His name.

Third, our petition should always reflect not our own will, but the will of the King, for the will of the King is law: *"Your kingdom come, Your will be done on earth as it is in heaven."* Remember, this is Jesus instructing His disciples how to pray. In other words, the King Himself is telling us what to ask Him for. He says nothing about cars or clothes or food. Instead, He says, "Petition for My government influence to come to Earth, for My intentions, purposes, culture, lifestyle, and will to be done on Earth just as they are in Heaven."

(Chapter Six)

Prayerfully and deliberately say the Lord's Prayer aloud to your God and King.

Day 23

PRAYING FOR YEAST

But seek first [God's] kingdom and [God's] righteousness, and all these things will be given to you as well (Matthew 6:33).

TODAY'S DEVOTION

IF you are one of those people who have trouble praying because you never know what to pray for, I have just destroyed your last excuse. You don't have to pray long as long as you pray right. Take the time every day—at your bedside when you first get up, in the shower, while getting dressed, driving to work, or whatever—pray simply, "Lord, let Your Kingdom come and let Your will be done in my life today as it is in Heaven." Start praying that prayer, and look for opportunities that God gives you for fulfilling it. Tend to God's business this way, and watch how He starts tending to yours.

Even Jesus' prayer for His followers in John chapter 17 is a "yeast" prayer:

> *My prayer is not that You take them out of the world but that You protect them from the evil one. They are not of the world, even as I am not of it. Sanctify them by the truth; Your word is truth. As You sent Me into the world, I have sent them into the world* (John 17:15-18).

(Chapter Six)

CONSIDERATIONS

1. When we focus our hearts and minds to pray for Heaven to come to Earth, then the next part of Jesus' Garden expansion prayer makes more sense: *"Give us today our daily bread"* (Matt. 6:11). What connection can you draw from this statement?

2. "Daily bread" certainly refers to food, but the ancient Jews also often used the word *bread* as an idiom that meant everything necessary for life. Do today's believers need more than physical nourishment when confronting challenges? Explain.

3. How can the yeast of His influence help us bring about His Kingdom expansion on Earth?

4. Name several differences between saying, "I am in business for myself for my own profit," or saying, "I am in His business for the sake of His influence."

5. We are not here to *escape*; we are here to *reshape*. Are there times when believers should take a stand about issues, circumstances, injustice? List a few.

MEDITATION

Many believers say, "I want a Christian job with a Christian boss in a Christian workplace." While there certainly are believers whom the Lord has called to such positions, He calls most of us to bloom and prosper right where we are, in the middle of the finance field, or the hotel field, or the food industry, or education, or government, because there is a whole lot of dough out there with a whole lot of needs. He wants us to infect the hospitality industry, banking, business, politics, sports, and so forth.

(Chapter Six)

Are believers effectively infecting their workplaces, communities, and families with the Kingdom? How about you?

Day 24

PRICELESS TREASURE

The kingdom of heaven is like treasure hidden in a field. When a man found it, he hid it again, and then in his joy went and sold all he had and bought that field.

Again, the kingdom of heaven is like a merchant looking for fine pearls. When he found one of great value, he went away and sold everything he had and bought it (Matthew 13:44-46).

TODAY'S DEVOTION

THESE parables speak of two different types of people and their responses to the Kingdom. The man in the first parable is like most of the people in the world, either searching aimlessly for they know not what, or simply going through life unaware of the priceless treasure at their feet until they stumble upon it (seemingly) by accident. This man may have heard a rumor of treasure in the field and gone looking for it, or he may simply have been crossing the field and come upon the treasure unexpectedly. Either way, the moment he found it, he knew it was what he had been seeking all his life. He immediately recognized its priceless value—and that it was worth any price he had to pay to obtain it. Accordingly, he sold everything he had and bought the field. The Kingdom of Heaven is far more valuable than anything this world has to offer.

In the second parable, the merchant knew what he was looking for: fine pearls. Finding one of "great value," he knew right away that in beauty and worth, it far outstripped any other pearl he had ever found, and he too sold everything he had in order to buy it.

Many people know they are searching for something, for some sense of meaning and purpose to life. Some even have at least a vague idea of what they want. They sample different religions, try out various philosophies, and comb through the world's wisdom literature looking for answers and searching for truth. Upon discovering the Kingdom (or being discovered by it), they know intuitively that here, finally, is the answer to all their questions and the end of their long quest.

(Chapter Six)

CONSIDERATIONS

1. In the two examples cited in Today's Devotion, which person do you more readily identify with? Why?

2. Although the Kingdom gives us access to all the riches of Heaven and all the resources of eternity, some people refuse to accept the King's free gifts. Why?

3. Entrance into the Kingdom of Heaven is open to all. The King excludes no one from His invitation to possess the priceless treasure. List several Scripture passages that confirm these statements.

4. The invigorating waters of Kingdom life are offered to all without cost or exclusion (see Isa. 55:1; Rev. 21:6), yet there will be many who exclude themselves by refusing to drink. Why?

5. God wants to invade Earth with Heaven, to infect Earth with Heaven's culture until Earth begins to look just like Heaven. How will He accomplish His plan?

MEDITATION

The ultimate power and goal of Garden influence is to develop a heavenly culture on Earth that produces a Kingdom community. God desires to build a heavenly community on Earth through the cultivation of His Kingdom culture here. This is demonstrated both in the prayer of Jesus: *"Your kingdom come, Your will be done on earth as it is in heaven"* (Matt. 6:10), and in the plan of God from the beginning: *"Let Us make man in Our image...and let them rule..."* (Gen. 1:26).

God doesn't want a religion. He doesn't want a weekend ceremony. He isn't looking for a group of weird people dressed in weird clothes saying weird things. God wants a holy community of whole and complete citizens, a community that represents and reflects Heaven on Earth, and He wants to do it through cultivating His Kingdom's culture on Earth through the lives and influence of His people.

(Chapter Six)

How committed are you to possessing the priceless treasure for your very own?

Day 25

PRIDE AND INDEPENDENCE

Sin entered the world through one man, and death through sin, and in this way death came to all men, because all sinned. ...Consequently, just as the result of one trespass was condemnation for all men, so also the result of one act of righteousness was justification that brings life for all men. For just as through the disobedience of the one man the many were made sinners, so also through the obedience of the one man the many will be made righteous (Romans 5:12,18-19).

TODAY'S DEVOTION

HUMAN history has demonstrated time and time again that as a race, we are manifestly incapable of governing ourselves effectively apart from the Spirit and principles of God. God, of course, knew this from the start, which is why, in the wake of man's rebellion, He set into motion His plan to reclaim, or recolonize the planet, a plan He established even before the foundations of the Earth were laid.

Recolonization is an unfamiliar concept because it is extremely rare for a colony, once it has declared its independence from a kingdom, to later change its mind and desire to return to colonial status. God, however, initiated the recolonization of Earth for two reasons: because His sovereign will and intent will never be thwarted; and because our survival as a race depends on it.

(Chapter Seven)

CONSIDERATIONS

1. A king is the governing authority over a territory. He impacts it with his will, purpose, and intent, producing a citizenry of people who reflect the king's morals, values, and lifestyle. What are the differences between a republic and a kingdom?

2. Why is living in a kingdom much more challenging than living in a democracy?

3. How is individuality looked upon in a kingdom? A democracy?

4. Why did God give Adam and Eve free will if He knew they would disobey Him?

5. Rebelling against the Kingdom is sin; sins are the day-to-day actions that constitute rebel-like behavior. How can believers stymie the rebellious nature within?

MEDITATION

Personal independence is the number one tenet of capitalism and democratic republics. The thing God hates is the very thing we magnify. The thing that God says is our condemnation is the very thing we regard as our highest achievement. As independent individuals, we can do whatever we like and pursue our own happiness and our own joy at our own expense. We take great pride in "doing our own thing"; but God says, "That's the very problem with the world." It's a paradox. This is why it is very difficult to live in the Kingdom of God and live at the same time in a democracy under a capitalistic system. It is hard to strike a balance between the two, because the principles by which they operate are diametrically opposed to each other.

(Chapter Seven)

Is your sense of pride and independence holding you back from receiving all that God has for you?

Day 26

"BRING THEM HERE TO ME"

Jesus replied, "They do not need to go away. You give them something to eat."

"We have here only five loaves of bread and two fish," they answered.

"Bring them here to Me," He said. And He directed the people to sit down on the grass. Taking the five loaves and the two fish and looking up to heaven, He gave thanks and broke the loaves. Then He gave them to the disciples, and the disciples gave them to the people. They all ate and were satisfied, and the disciples picked up twelve basketfuls of broken pieces that were left over. The number of those who ate was about five thousand men, besides women and children (Matthew 14:16-21).

TODAY'S DEVOTION

CULTURE reflects government. In the world's culture, some people go hungry. Some people are poor or sick or lacking some of the basic necessities for a high quality of life. Inequities abound and injustice is rampant. Not in Kingdom culture. Wherever Jesus went, sick people were made well—because there is no sickness in the Kingdom. Hungry people were fed and satisfied—because there is no hunger or lack of any kind in the Kingdom.

When 5,000 people in a remote place needed to be fed, Jesus did the natural thing (from the Kingdom perspective)—He fed them. His disciples wanted to send the people away to buy food because they were approaching the situation from a point of view of lack. Jesus, however, knew there was no lack because

He had unlimited access to the unlimited resources of His Father's Kingdom. (See John 6:5-13.)

When Jesus took those five loaves and two fish from His disciples, He took them out of the economy of His day and into Kingdom-ism. Once inside that new economy, the very atoms in that fish and bread began to behave differently. What we call a miracle was simply normal activity in the Kingdom. And it should be normal activity for all who manifest Kingdom culture.

(Chapter Seven)

CONSIDERATIONS

1. When Kingdom living prevails, afflictions such as hunger, fear, discouragement, defeat, curses, and greed do not exist. List other maladies that do not exist in Heaven's culture on Earth.

2. Jesus' disciples struggled when learning how to shift their thinking and their behavior from the worldly culture of their birth to the Kingdom culture. What is one of the most difficult behaviors you have had to shift your thinking about? Have you been successful?

3. Jesus challenges our behavior, beliefs, values, thoughts, perceptions, assumptions, and expectations. Yet it is only through the power of the Holy Spirit that believers can change their worldly culture and traditions: Is this statement true or false? Why?

4. In the same way that there are Chinatown subcultures within larger city cultures, have you built a Kingdom subculture within your larger workplace or neighborhood culture?

5. Are believers worldwide receiving the kind of attention that Jesus did when He was spreading Kingdom culture? Why or why not?

MEDITATION

People should be able to walk into our presence or into our homes or churches and feel like they have walked into another country. They should be able to tell immediately by our language, dress, manners, attitude, and behavior that we are not of this world. Our culture should stand out so clearly that no one can mistake it.

Life with Jesus was always this way, which is why He attracted so much attention. People either loved Him or hated Him, accepted Him or rejected Him; but no one ignored Him. Everywhere He went He brought Kingdom culture. Throngs of people surrounded Him because He showed them the power, quality, nature, and irresistible appeal of a culture that could make them victors in life rather than victims—and then He told them how to achieve it.

(Chapter Seven)

Jesus caused a commotion wherever He went. Are you stirring up reactions by taking Kingdom culture to your school, workplace, church?

CULTURE REVELATIONS (PART I)

[Jesus said], *"You have heard that it was said, 'Love your neigh-bor and hate your enemy.' But I tell you: Love your enemies and pray for those who persecute you, that you may be sons of your Father in heaven"* (Matthew 5:43-45a).

TODAY'S DEVOTION

CULTURE is the total life of a people passed on to their descendants. Culture is an extremely powerful thing. Its roots grow deep and its influence reaches far. This is why a group of people bound together by culture can live for generations in a country not their own and still maintain their distinct identity. Culture encompasses the totality of life: dress, food, drink, customs, manners, etiquette, protocol, attitudes toward children and the elderly, religious beliefs, ethical and moral values, social norms, and both public and private behavior.

If we are manifesting Kingdom culture in our lives, people who meet us should be able to say, "I think I just entered Heaven. You don't lie, you don't cheat, you don't steal, you don't sleep around, you've been married to the same person for 30 years; what's up with you? Where are you from? Why are you so different?" When people outside the Kingdom look at Kingdom citizens or a

Kingdom community, they should see a culture distinctly different—and much more attractive—from their own.

(Chapter Seven)

CONSIDERATIONS

Culture reveals itself in at least 16 specific ways. Write a short definition for the following eight characteristics, applying them to your personal experiences:

Values:

Priorities:

Behaviors:

Standards:

Celebrations:

Morality:

Relationships:

Ethics:

MEDITATION

The character of a nation's culture is revealed in the ethical standards it practices. These may be quite different from the "official" standards established by law for ethical behavior. Many corrupt and unethical governments have given lip service to the highest ethical standards, even as their leaders victimized the people and plundered the treasury for their own enrichment. Corruption as the moral fabric of a culture guarantees the poverty of a nation, not only economically but morally and spiritually as well.

(Chapter Seven)

How has defining these eight characteristics of culture expanded your view of Kingdom culture?

CULTURE REVELATIONS (PART 2)

Make sure that nobody pays back wrong for wrong, but always try to be kind to each other and to everyone else. Be joyful always; pray continually; give thanks in all circumstances, for this is God's will for you in Christ Jesus. Do not put out the Spirit's fire; do not treat prophecies with contempt. Test everything. Hold onto the good. Avoid every kind of evil (I Thessalonians 5:15-22).

TODAY'S DEVOTION

CULTURE also reveals itself in the attitude of the people. There are certain countries you can visit where the people are very warm and friendly; they are appreciative of visitors and go out of their way to make them feel welcome. I love visiting places like that. At the other end of the spectrum are those countries where the people in general are rude, arrogant, or superior in their demeanor, where even people in the "service" industries such as hotels and restaurants act as though they are insulted by your presence and that they are doing you a favor by serving you.

No one should ever feel unwelcome when they enter a place where Kingdom culture is present. On the contrary, they should feel as though they have entered Heaven itself. This is why the Bible says, "Let love prevail among you." That is the culture of Heaven. "Let forgiveness prevail among you." That is the culture of Heaven. "Let joy unspeakable prevail among you." That is the culture of Heaven. "Let the peace that passes understanding prevail among you." That is the culture of Heaven.

(Chapter Seven)

CONSIDERATIONS

As mentioned in yesterday's devotion, culture reveals itself in at least 16 specific ways. Write a short definition for the following eight characteristics, applying them to your personal experiences:

Social norms:

Attitudes:

Dress:

Food:

Responses:

Drink:

Whatever is permitted:

Whatever is accepted:

MEDITATION

Community means essentially that individuality is gone and everybody lives and works for the good of everybody else. Western society, with its emphasis on independence and individualism, has largely lost touch with the concept of community, and this has affected many churches and believers. The time has come for Kingdom citizens to rediscover and reclaim community as an essential part of

Kingdom life; this is critical to the successful reproduction of Kingdom gardens throughout the Earth. After all, a Kingdom community is a Kingdom garden.

(Chapter Seven)

How has defining these eight characteristics of culture expanded your view of Kingdom culture?

Day 29

DREAMING

"For My thoughts are not your thoughts, neither are your ways My ways,"
declares the Lord. "As the heavens are higher than the earth, so are My ways
higher than your ways and My thoughts than your thoughts"(Isaiah 55:8-9).

TODAY'S DEVOTION

I HAVE a dream that before I die I will see and be part of a dynamic, grow-ing community of people among whom there is no sickness, no poverty, and no want. Everyone will be debt-free. Depression, worry, and despair will be unknown; every marriage will be strong, successful, and happy; and all the children will respect their parents and live completely free of fear. The entire community will worship the Lord in perfect unity and harmony, and with a single common vision.

People from outside will be amazed at what they see. "Do you mean that out of these 50,000 people, nobody is divorced? Why not?"

"Because in our community we don't believe in that. We believe in fix-ing things up, in repenting, reconciling, and forgiving. That's our nature, our culture."

"Do you mean to tell me that among these 200,000 people there is no incest? How can this be?"

"Because in our community such a thing is detestable. We love our children. They are made in God's image and we care for and protect them. That's our culture."

"Do you mean to tell me that out of half a million people, nobody tells lies?"

"It's true. Lying is unheard of in our community. Truth is our currency. In our community, truth is not the best policy—it is the only policy."

I dream of the day when this will be reality. Fantasy, you say? Utopia? No, simply Kingdom culture in action.

(Chapter Eight)

CONSIDERATIONS

1. We dream of Heaven because we can't find the community we want here on Earth. Describe a few life circumstances that make believers dream of Heaven rather than face situations.

2. Why is the concept of Heaven on Earth so hard to accept?

3. What will it take for believers to stop dreaming about Heaven and to embrace a Kingdom mindset?

4. God's purpose has always been to build a heavenly community on Earth, a community that would reflect in the physical realm the:

    _____, _____,

    _____, _____,

    _____, and _____

    character of His Kingdom in the spiritual realm.

5. The word *community* comes from the words "common" and "unity." It refers to a group of people who share a common language,

food, dress, lifestyle, customs, values, and morals. Name a few commonalities that bind your neighborhood or church together.

MEDITATION

Our assignment as Kingdom citizens and ambassadors is to learn—and then teach others—how to apply the Kingdom to business and bodily health; to single life, marriage, and parenting; to investments and speech; to relationships and professions; and to government and media. We have to reintroduce the precepts of the Kingdom of Heaven, the values, morals, principles, and standards by which our society is supposed to live. God's plan, then, is not—and never has been—to establish a religious institution, but to build a living, breathing, and thriving community that reveals to the world what He is like as well as the quality of life under His government.

(Chapter Eight)

Dreaming about Heaven isn't wrong, but living for God's glory now within the Kingdom of Heaven is His desire for us. Are you dreaming or living?

REFLECTED GLORY

*When the queen of Sheba heard about the fame of Solomon and his relation
to the name of the Lord, she came to test him with hard questions. Arriving
at Jerusalem with a very great caravan—with camels carrying spices, large
quantities of gold, and precious stones—she came to Solomon and talked with
him about all that she had on her mind. Solomon answered all her questions;
nothing was too hard for the king to explain to her. . . .*

*She said to the king, "The report I heard in my own country about your
achievements and your wisdom is true. But I did not believe these things
until I came and saw them with my own eyes. Indeed, not even half was
told me; in wisdom and wealth you have far exceeded the report I heard"*
(I Kings 10:1-3,6-7).

TODAY'S DEVOTION

THE purpose behind a Kingdom community is to reflect the greatness
and glory of the King. Citizens of the community are under the rule of
the King and come to manifest His nature. In other words, the people take on
the characteristics of the King, display the qualities of the King, and exhibit the
culture of the King. As a matter of fact, the quality and nature of any kingdom
can be recognized first not by the presence of the king but by the lifestyle of
his citizens. Seeing how the people in a kingdom live reveals a great deal about
their king.

That's how kingdoms work. Kingdoms are manifested in the culture of the people. So the quality of the community is a manifestation or reflection of the quality of the king.

(Chapter Eight)

CONSIDERATIONS

1. In your opinion, are the believers in the Western world reflective of God's glory? Why or why not?

2. What are five steps that believers can take to better reflect the glory of God's love and tender mercy?

3. What does your reputation say about your role as a child of the King? Do people immediately know that you are not of this world?

4. When you are born into wealth, you don't talk about wealth. God's ultimate goal is to bring that kind of life on Earth. Why is it hard for believers to accept the wealth of the Kingdom that God freely offers to them?

5. What is the difference between living within walls of latex and walls of gold?

MEDITATION

When we pray for the Kingdom, our prayer encompasses all we could ever need or desire, because with the Kingdom comes access to everything—all the resources of Heaven. This is why Jesus also told us not to worry about what we would eat, drink, or wear, or about any other thing, but to seek first the Kingdom and righteousness of God, for with the Kingdom comes everything else. Our future is tied up in the culture of the King. Therefore our prayer should be, "Lord, let Your Kingdom be manifested in us. Make us into a community that represents Your country and Your culture. May our common unity be a reflection of Your glory to a watching world."

(Chapter Eight)

Sincerely pray this prayer again—and commit it to your daily devotions.

Day 31

COMMUNITY =
COMMON UNITY

I in them and You in Me. May they be brought to complete unity to let the world know that You sent Me and have loved them even as You have loved Me (John 17:23).

May the God who gives endurance and encouragement give you a spirit of unity among yourselves as you follow Christ Jesus (Romans 15:5).

Make every effort to keep the unity of the Spirit through the bond of peace (Ephesians 4:3).

Today's Devotion

CHINATOWN is a community. Its inhabitants are united by the common bond of their Chinese heritage and culture, which they keep vibrantly alive. Chinatown could never exist with only one or two or just a handful of Chinese. Maintaining a distinct cultural identity requires a large number of people of similar background working together in a common purpose. In Los Angeles, the population of Chinatown is around 500,000 people. They speak their own language, worship in their own temples, operate their own businesses, and maintain their own distinctive cuisine. Theirs is a distinct and unmistakably unique community, a "garden" of China within the United States.

Kingdom communities, wherever they are in the world, should be just as unique and distinctive. Our values, standards, beliefs, norms, language, customs, traditions, and ideals should set us apart from the rest of the world. People who walk into our community should feel like they have stepped into Heaven.

(Chapter Eight)

CONSIDERATIONS

1. Why is it impossible for "religious" Christianity to take the place of the Kingdom?

2. Religious Christianity looks nothing like Heaven. Why?

3. The Kingdom of Heaven is bigger than our _____, and broader than our _____. Explain.

4. Can you envision a community on Earth where people forgive one another, love their enemies, do good to those who mistreat them, never engage in slander or gossip, are honest, and respect the dignity of others? Why or why not?

5. What must happen first before fallen humankind can assume a common ideology or philosophy with the King of kings?

MEDITATION

Can you see Heaven's culture coming to Earth? Can you imagine a community where every husband loves his wife the way Christ loves His Church, and treats her like the queen she is? Can you imagine a community where every wife honors, respects, and builds up her husband? Can you imagine a community where husbands and wives are absolutely faithful to each other and where adultery or sweethearting is inconceivable? Can you imagine a community where all the children honor and obey their parents and show respect to all legitimate authority? Can you imagine a community where people's word is their bond and where honesty is the common currency? Can you imagine a community where there is no cursing or gambling, no greed or thievery, no envy or jealousy, no backbiting or backstabbing, no petty bickering or quarreling, and no lust or sexual immorality? Can you imagine a community where there is no poverty or want, but abundant peace and contentment? Can you imagine it? God can, and this is the type of community He wants to fill the Earth with.

(Chapter Eight)

Take a few minutes to close your eyes and imagine living in a community where God's love permeates all.

A LESSON TO LEARN

If Your Presence does not go with us, do not send us up from here. How will anyone know that You are pleased with me and with Your people unless You go with us? What else will distinguish me and Your people from all the other people on the face of the earth? (Exodus 33:15b-16)

TODAY'S DEVOTION

IF there is any group of people on Earth who understand the power of community, it is the Jews. Through 4,000 years of war and conquest, peace and prosperity, persecution and prejudice, and triumph and tragedy, the Jews have maintained a distinct cultural identity as a people. This is due in large part to the fact that they identify themselves not only as individuals but also as interdependent members of a larger community.

The first five books of the Bible are political books, not religious treatises. They explain how God's purpose for delivering the Israelites from slavery in Egypt was to transform them into a nation through whom He would bless the world, just as He had promised Abraham (see Gen. 12:1-3). According to God's plan, they would be a distinct people, separate from the other nations of the world in their worship, their laws, their morality, their diet, their code of conduct, and their everyday lifestyle. The distinguishing characteristic that would set them apart from other peoples would be God's active and continuing presence among them.

(Chapter Eight)

CONSIDERATIONS

1. The active and powerful presence of God in our everyday lives and activities distinguishes believers from other people. How?

2. Members of Jewish communities help each other. Why don't believers and followers of Christ do the same? We have no sense of community. Why?

3. As Kingdom citizens we are a community, and we are dependent on one another. How is today's community of believers different from those of the first-century church?

4. Some communities publish directories of local and regional businesses and services owned by believers. Why should believers consider patronizing only these businesses?

5. What are some of the advantages of establishing a Christian-based community where everyone is committed to serving God and each other?

MEDITATION

As a Kingdom community, we are held to a higher standard than that of the world. Religious communities often adapt and conform to the world's standards, which is one reason they are such a mess. Kingdom communities, on the other hand, do not accommodate; they elevate. They hold out the standards of the King without compromise, and elevate to that level all who enter. That's the only way it can be.

In a Kingdom community, Kingdom citizens have no independent life. This is a particularly hard concept to grasp for those who have grown up under democratic and capitalistic systems where personal independence is regarded as one of the highest values of all. As Kingdom citizens, we are all in this together.

We need each other. We are all members of one Body and every member is vital for the proper functioning of that Body. That is why an "illness" that infects one of us infects all of us. And that is why we cannot afford to ignore or write off any member of the community.

(Chapter Eight)

What lesson can you learn from the Jewish mindset about community? Think of ways you can infuse this lesson within your Christian community.

THE PRINCIPLE OF ENGAGEMENT

Then the righteous will answer Him, "Lord, when did we see You hungry and feed You, or thirsty and give You something to drink? When did we see You a stranger and invite You in, or needing clothes and clothe You? When did we see you sick or in prison and go to visit You?"

The King will reply, "I tell you the truth, whatever you did for one of the least of these brothers of Mine, you did for Me" (Matthew 25:37-40).

TODAY'S DEVOTION

WE have not inherited a religion. Cultures and societies may transfer religions from one generation to the next, but that is not our inheritance. Our inheritance is the Kingdom—not just any kingdom, but *the* Kingdom. What Adam lost, Christ has restored to us. Rulership is in our genes, authority in our very makeup. We were designed to rule the Earth. The Kingdom is the rightful inheritance of all humankind. Many people, however, do not know this, which is why we of the Kingdom community must engage those who live in the world's culture. They need to be informed of their inheritance.

As Kingdom citizens, our goal should be to stay in touch with Heaven every moment of every day. It is for this reason that God sent His Holy Spirit, not to visit us but to live inside of us, so He could guide us into the knowledge of all truth and teach us how to live and act and talk like the King.

This is the way—and the only way—for us to exert a continuing influence and make a permanent impact for the Kingdom in the popular culture. In order to transform the popular culture, we must *engage* the popular culture; and we can engage it successfully only in the Spirit, likeness, and power of our King.

(Chapter Nine)

CONSIDERATIONS

1. The Kingdom principle of engagement is simply defined as influencing the popular culture through the community of faith. List a few examples of how this principle can be implemented within a local community, state, and nation.

2. As Kingdom citizens and members of the Kingdom community, we not only possess the answer to humanity's search for meaning, but we also bear the responsibility of sharing it with others. How have you found to be the best way to share the Good News with others?

3. Are most Christians in Western nations committed to representing the nature and character of our King, and to living His culture daily before the world with boldness, and without apology or compromise?

4. The King desires for every person in the world to become a citizen of His community and to receive his or her inheritance. Influencing popular culture where you live causes a wide-reaching ripple effect. How and why?

5. To transform the popular culture, we must _____ the popular culture, and we can _____ it successfully only in the Spirit, likeness, and power of our King.

MEDITATION

Although we will not experience the complete fullness of our inheritance until we enter the life to come, as Kingdom citizens our inheritance is a present reality. In fact, Kingdom community life is the daily living out of our inheritance in real and practical ways.

(Chapter Nine)

Jesus told His disciples, *"Feed My sheep"* (John 21:17). Think of three ways you can feed His sheep. Choose one and put your thoughts into action.

Day 34

HEAVEN IS NOT OUR PRIORITY (PART 1)

The highest heavens belong to the Lord, but the earth He has given to man (Psalm 115:16).

TODAY'S DEVOTION

WHEN talking about the Kingdom principle of engagement, it is important that we first understand what our assignment is *not*. Because there is so much confusion on this issue, we need to be absolutely clear about what we are not supposed to do.

Just as Heaven is not our priority, the world is not our enemy. Although as Kingdom citizens we are not *of* the world, we are *in* the world, and it is God's will that we engage the world's culture with the principles, claims, and authority of the Kingdom of Heaven.

(Chapter Nine)

CONSIDERATIONS

Describe your thoughts about the following statements:

1. God did not assign us to go to Heaven.

2. God did not assign us to prepare others to go to Heaven.

3. God did not assign us to establish a religion.

4. God did not assign us to promote a religion or a denomination.

5. God did not assign us to separate or isolate ourselves from the world.

MEDITATION

We cannot engage the popular culture by escaping from it, nor can we influence it by isolating ourselves from it. Jesus certainly didn't. One of the biggest criticisms the religious leaders leveled against Jesus was the fact that He spent so much time with "sinners," the dirty, disreputable, and cast-off dregs of society. When challenged on this, He responded,

> *It is not the healthy who need a doctor, but the sick. But go and learn what this means: 'I desire mercy, not sacrifice.' For I have not come to call the righteous, but sinners* (Matthew 9:12-13).

That is our assignment too.

(Chapter Nine)

Heaven is not our priority—spreading the Kingdom of God on Earth is!

HEAVEN IS NOT OUR PRIORITY (PART 2)

The highest heavens belong to the Lord, but the earth He has given to man (Psalm 115:16).

TODAY'S DEVOTION

WE accomplish nothing by attacking and condemning people for their sins. Deep in their hearts, unbelievers know they are sinners. They know their lives are messed up and out of alignment with God. They don't need us in our self-righteousness laying it out for them, especially if we come off sounding like we think we are beyond those kinds of things. They know better. We can't draw people to the Kingdom by offending them with our manner. (Becoming offended by our message, however, is another matter entirely.) In order to influence them, we must show patience and sensitivity.

There is no need for us to "defend" the Kingdom; that is not our job. The King is perfectly capable of defending His own Kingdom. Our assignment is not to compete with the world, because there is no competition. We are from a different country than those who are of the world. Our job is not to compete, but to manifest the Kingdom in our lives, and let the Kingdom speak for itself.

(Chapter Nine)

CONSIDERATIONS

1. God did not assign us to attack or condemn the world.

   Describe your thoughts about this statement.

2. God did not assign us to compete with the world.

   Describe your thoughts about this statement.

3. God did not assign us to avoid the world.

   Describe your thoughts about this statement.

4. Does it seem as if believers are trying to compete with the world? List several ways you've witnessed this competition.

5. Because of the escapist mentality taught by many churches, many believers have virtually written off any chance or effort of trying to change the world. Why is this reasoning faulty?

MEDITATION

As Kingdom citizens, we are in the world for a reason: not to avoid the world, but to do our part to influence and change the world through our personal involvement. Run for the school board so you can help monitor what kinds of textbooks come into the classrooms in your community. Get involved in politics. Run for office, or at the very least, vote regularly. Read up on current issues and stay abreast of the news. Choose a "secular" career that will get you into the mainstream of society where your influence can be the greatest. Get involved in education. Get involved in business. Get involved in entertainment. Get involved in every area of law and medicine. We cannot engage the popular culture by avoiding it; we must fill it with Kingdom people.

(Chapter Nine)

Is God calling you to step out into a new area for Him? Trust that He will give you all the talent, skill, and encouragement you need to succeed!

Day 36

ENGAGING THE WORLD

You are the salt of the earth. But if the salt loses its saltiness, how can it be made salty again? It is no longer good for anything, except to be thrown out and trampled by men.

You are the light of the world. A city set on a hill cannot be hidden. Neither do people light a lamp and put it under a bowl. Instead they put it on its stand, and it gives light to everyone in the house. In the same way, let your light shine before men, that they may see your good deeds and praise your Father in heaven (Matthew 5:13-16).

TODAY'S DEVOTION

GOD did not place us on Earth as His people just so we could start getting ready to leave. He placed us here to plant and reproduce gardens of His Kingdom throughout the world, thereby reclaiming and transforming territory laid waste by the pretender's rapacious rule.

Religion separates and isolates. The Kingdom engages. Just as a farmer sows his seed, so the King sprinkles His Kingdom citizens everywhere with an abundant harvest in mind. He is saying, "I am throwing you out; wherever you land, infect that place for Me. Don't isolate yourself. Don't stay away from folks who are not in the Kingdom. Get involved. Engage. Make an impact where you are. Be bold in My strength to confront the earthly powers of this present age. The world will soon see who is more powerful." The Kingdom of Heaven is not afraid of evil, and we who are its citizens need not fear it either, because the One who is in us is greater than the one who is in the world (see I John 4:4).

(Chapter Nine)

CONSIDERATIONS

I. Write a brief thought about each of the following statements:

God assigned us to reintroduce the Kingdom to the world.

God assigned us to repossess the Earth with the Kingdom.

God assigned us to engage the world system.

God assigned us to influence the world, not to keep up with it.

2. Write a brief thought about each of the following statements:

God assigned us to infect the world, not reject the world.

God assigned us to revolutionize the world.

God assigned us to occupy the Earth, not abandon it.

God assigned us to promote the government of Heaven on Earth.

MEDITATION

As Jesus explained to His disciples, the man who sowed the good seed represents the Son of Man, Jesus Himself; the enemy who sowed the weeds is the devil; the good seed represents children of the Kingdom, and the weeds, children of the devil (see Matt. 13:37-39).

The point I want us to understand here is that the wheat and the weeds—the children of the Kingdom and the children of the devil—are allowed to *grow together* until the harvest, which takes place at the end of time. In other words,

Kingdom citizens *mingle* with citizens of the world throughout history, and this is by the King's design. He has chosen deliberately to leave His children in the world, in the midst of the "weeds," so that we can make a difference in the lives of those weeds.

In strictly human terms, we all know that a weed cannot change into a stalk of wheat, but in God's Kingdom nothing is impossible. By His power working in and through the lives and influence of His people, God can convert useless weeds into purposeful wheat. He can transform dark, confused, broken, and unproductive people into persons full of purpose, abundant life, and fulfilled destiny. But He cannot work through us for this purpose unless we are in the world and among the weeds. That is the concept behind the Kingdom principle of engagement.

(Chapter Nine)

How willing are you to engage some weeds for the purpose of establishing His Garden?

LIVING IN TWO WORLDS

Your kingdom is an everlasting kingdom, and Your dominion endures through all generations (Psalm 145:13a).

TODAY'S DEVOTION

KINGDOM citizens are people with their feet in two different worlds. One foot is planted squarely in the Kingdom community, where daily life is ordered by the righteous principles, standards, and culture of God Almighty, while the other stands securely in the society and culture of the world. At heart, the two worlds are incompatible because they operate according to principles and philosophies that are diametrically opposed to each other. Yet we live in both worlds simultaneously. This is the challenge of living in the Kingdom. In order to do so successfully, we have to understand the principle of Kingdom extension and influence and how it works in conjunction with the present culture we are in. How do we live in two worlds on one Earth? More importantly, how do we claim one world—the popular culture—and bring it under Kingdom government?

Attitude is the key, and attitude determines strategy.

(Chapter Ten)

CONSIDERATIONS

1. List a few times when you felt as if you had one foot in the Kingdom of Heaven and the other foot in the world's kingdom.

2. Whenever we pray, "Your kingdom come, and Your will be done on earth as it is in heaven," we are praying for the celestial to transform the terrestrial. Describe what this means to you.

3. As children of God created in His image and likeness, we have firm connections to the celestial and the terrestrial. How do these connections enhance or detract from our connection with God?

4. One of the first attitude adjustments we must make is to get rid of our 'religious' thinking. Why?

5. In what ways can believers prepare themselves for the inevitable clash of the two worlds they live in?

MEDITATION

All who are Kingdom citizens face the dilemma and challenge of how to live successfully and simultaneously in two worlds that are in inevitable conflict. In Chapter Two we talked about the clash of cultures between the Kingdom and the world. One critical key to our successful navigation within these two worlds is to get it thoroughly into our heads that the Kingdom of Heaven is not a kingdom of coexistence but of transformation, and that it is the Kingdom, not the world, that will ultimately prevail. This understanding can help us develop the habit of thinking with a Kingdom mindset and making Kingdom decisions in every area of life.

As Kingdom citizens, we must be prepared for clash and conflict. We cannot enter the Kingdom of God and continue to live like our unsaved friends. All of a sudden everything changes: our culture, our nature, our interests, our priorities, our tastes—everything. We are new creations in Christ; the old is gone and everything has become new (see 2 Cor. 5:17). Our assignment on Earth is not coexistence, compromise, or half measures. It is total transformation. It is love taking over a love-starved planet.

(Chapter Ten)

Most people try to avoid conflict—are you prepared for the inevitable?

Day 38

TRANSFORMATION

Do not conform any longer to the pattern of this world, but be transformed by the renewing of your mind (Romans 12:2a).

TODAY'S DEVOTION

WHENEVER the Kingdom comes into a place, it impacts and overrides the culture of that place, not with violence or heavy-handed tactics, but with love and an unshakable confidence in the absolute legitimacy, superiority, and supremacy of Kingdom government. We are not supposed to dress like the popular culture, or live like the popular culture, or take a light view of sex and morality like the popular culture. We are supposed to set the standard, the higher standard of the Kingdom. We are supposed to override the popular culture. We are supposed to exercise self-control and moderation in all things and impact the people around us. We should not allow the environment to change us.

Instead, we should change our environment and bring it into conformity with God's Kingdom. The apostle Paul said, *"Do not conform any longer to the pattern of this world, but be transformed by the renewing of your mind"* (Rom. 12:2a). Once transformed in this manner, we then transform our environment wherever we go, until it is a clear reflection of the Kingdom.

(Chapter Ten)

CONSIDERATIONS

1. Fill in the blanks according to the differences between God's Kingdom and the kingdom of the world:

   Example: Sexual purity/Immorality

   Respect /_____

   Order/_____

   Honesty/_____

   Truthfulness/_____

   Love/_____

   Peace/_____

   Freedom/_____

2. Transformation of the popular culture will come only from communities of Kingdom citizens who refuse to remain silent. What are two topics you can speak out about and make a positive difference?

3. We must become proactive in reproducing Garden communities of the Kingdom wherever we are and wherever we go in the future. How will today's Garden communities be different from the Garden of Eden?

4. In Chapter Ten's example about the manager who turned a failing restaurant into a success, name five things that she did to transform the business. Were lives transformed as well? Who and why?

5. Transformation begins with you. How can you transform yourself, your family, your neighborhood, your church, your state, and your nation for His glory? Write at least one idea for each area.

MEDITATION

Being in the world but not of the world is not coexistence. Transformation of the popular culture will come only from communities of Kingdom citizens who refuse to remain silent or to sit idly by, uninvolved and disengaged, while the agents of the *"powers of this dark world and. . .the spiritual forces of evil in the heavenly realms"* (Eph. 6:12) set their agendas and run the show. We must speak up. We must step out. We must get involved. We must become proactive in reproducing garden communities of the Kingdom wherever we are and wherever we go in the future. That is our calling, and our assignment from the One who commanded us to *"go and make disciples of all nations, baptizing them in the name of the Father and of the Son and of the Holy Spirit, and teaching them to obey everything I have commanded you"* (Matt. 28:19-20a).

(Chapter Ten)

Transforming from the inside out is the biggest challenge—start today.

Then start on the outside tomorrow.

Day 39

A JUST AND
RIGHTEOUS KING

No good tree bears bad fruit, nor does a bad tree bear good fruit. Each tree is recognized by its own fruit. People do not pick figs from thornbushes, or grapes from briers. The good man brings good things out of the good stored up in his heart, and the evil man brings evil things out of the evil stored up in his heart. For out of the overflow of his heart his mouth speaks (Luke 6:43-45).

TODAY'S DEVOTION

HUMAN history is replete with examples of good kings and bad kings, good kingdoms and bad kingdoms, benevolent governments and oppressive governments. One fact that stands out clearly is this: As the king goes, so goes the kingdom. Since a kingdom is tied so closely to the nature and character of its king, it is virtually impossible for a good kingdom to come from a bad king, or a bad kingdom to come from a good king.

Fortunately for all of us, the King of kings is a good King, and His Kingdom is a good kingdom. That is why we who are citizens of the Kingdom of Heaven can live and work for the Kingdom—and engage the popular culture with it—in complete confidence that we are serving not only God, but also the better interests of our fellow humans who are not yet in the Kingdom. Our King's rule is just and righteous. He rules with fairness, grace, compassion, mercy, and, most of all, love. And in His love He delights to give all good things to His children, His people.

(Chapter Ten)

CONSIDERATIONS

1. How does our King of kings differ from kings of this world, be they unscrupulous CEOs, territorial dictators, dishonest managers, drunken spouses, etc.?

2. Jesus said, *"Do not be afraid, little flock, for your Father has been pleased to give you the kingdom."* Why did He preface His statement with *"Do not be afraid"*? What are people afraid of?

3. A depraved king's kingdom will be characterized by _____, _____, and _____.

4. The wealth of a kingdom will be reflected in the lifestyle of its people. If the kingdom is rich and the king is good, the people will be well off. Describe your lifestyle and quality of life as a citizen of the Kingdom of God.

5. Jesus says to you, *"Come to Me, all you who are weary and burdened, and I will give you rest. Take My yoke upon you and learn from Me, for I am gentle and humble in heart, and you will find rest for your souls. For My yoke is easy and My burden is light"* (Matt. 11:28-30). Does this Scripture bring you peace and comfort? Write about it.

MEDITATION

The King has the power and the ability to give rest to everyone who comes to Him—including all 7 billion plus of us on the face of the Earth. This is not some sweet and sentimental religious statement; it is a legal Kingdom decree.

"Come to Me, all 7 billion and more of you; I can heal you all, house you all, feed you all, dress you all, and bless you all—and still have as many resources as when I began."

Jesus is a good King, and His Kingdom is just what the world needs, which is why He wants to fill the Earth with His Kingdom communities, and use His citizens to do it.

(Chapter Ten)

Living for a just and righteous King gives you purpose, hope, and lasting joy. Start living for Him today.

Day 40

VICTORY THROUGH SERVICE

Jesus said to them, "You will indeed drink from My cup, but to sit at My right or left is not for Me to grant. These places belong to those for whom they have been prepared by My Father."

When the ten heard about this, they were indignant with the two brothers. Jesus called them together and said, "You know that the rulers of the Gentiles lord it over them, and their high officials exercise authority over them. Not so with you. Instead, whoever wants to become great among you must be your servant, and whoever wants to be first must be your slave—just as the Son of Man did not come to be served, but to serve, and to give His life as a ransom for many" (Matthew 20:23-28).

TODAY'S DEVOTION

NOTICE the progression above in Matthew 20:28: Jesus became a servant, and then He gave Himself. By His example He is telling us: "Find your gift and serve it to the world. That is how you will infect people with the Kingdom." If you set your heart on the Kingdom of Heaven and your sights on serving others in the King's name, He will open doors of opportunity for you that would never open otherwise. He will take you to places you would never be able to go on your own, and enable you to impact lives you would never even come close to touching any other way. He will take you to personal heights of joy, prosperity, and contentment beyond your wildest dreams and give you a broader influence in your world than you have ever imagined. But those things come not by seeking them, but by seeking Him; not by seeking the gifts, but by seeking the Giver.

(Chapter Ten)

CONSIDERATIONS

1. To expand God's Kingdom, believers must not use tactics of the world, such as self-promotion or selfish ambition. What principles should we use instead?

2. Define *self-abasement* and *servanthood.*

3. List five things that will happen if you set your heart on the Kingdom of Heaven and your sights on serving others in the King's name:

4. Setting aside your own ambitions and surrendering to His will for your life opens opportunities you never imagined. Do you have a secret desire that God has placed in your heart? Write it down.

5. *"Every good and perfect gift is from above, coming down from the Father of the heavenly lights, who does not change like shifting shadows"* (James 1:17).

Discover, define, and refine your gift from God—then give it away as part of planting His gardens.

Describe the gift(s) God has given you to share with others.

MEDITATION

Everyone dreams of being great, and there is nothing evil in that desire. We all want to be part of something significant. This is perfectly natural. Such a desire comes from God, because He created us for greatness, but we lost it when we lost the Kingdom. We can get it back, but not by walking on top of people, pushing people down, lording it over people, conniving, scheming, lying, stealing, or dealing under the table. Those are the ways of the world. In God's Kingdom, if you want to be great, you first must become the servant of all.

God's big idea was to extend His kingly influence and culture from the celestial to the terrestrial by planting garden communities throughout the Earth that would perfectly reflect the richness and abundant life of His heavenly Kingdom. And He chose to do it through citizen-servants like you and me who will seek first His Kingdom and His righteousness and live exclusively for Him—by humbling ourselves and giving ourselves freely to others so that they may see Him in us, learn of His Kingdom from us, and apply for citizenship themselves.

(Chapter Ten)

God's big idea includes you!

Accept His invitation to become the royal heir of His Kingdom, now and forever.

ABOUT
DR. MYLES MUNROE

DR. Myles Munroe is founder, president, and senior pastor of Bahamas Faith Ministries International. He is also founder and chairman of the International Third World Leaders Association and president of International Leadership Training Institute. He is respected internationally as a best-selling author, lecturer, teacher, coach, and leadership mentor. As a speaker, he has empowered many to discover their personal purpose and develop their true potential. He and his wife, Ruth, have two children, Charisa and Myles "Chairo" Jr. They reside in Nassau the Bahamas.

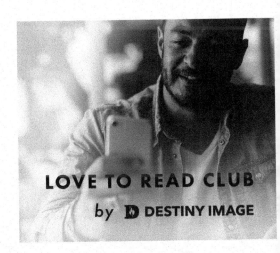